FISH & SEAFOOD

by
Jean Paré

Dedication

A tasty catch!

Cover Photo

FISH & SEAFOOD

First Printing April 1996

ISBN 1-895455-03-0

Published and Distributed by
Company's Coming Publishing Limited
Box 8037, Station "F"
Edmonton, Alberta, Canada
T6H 4N9

**Published Simultaneously in
Canada and the United States of America**

Printed In Canada

Company's Coming Cookbooks
by Jean Paré

COMPANY'S COMING SERIES
English

- 150 DELICIOUS SQUARES
- CASSEROLES
- MUFFINS & MORE
- SALADS
- APPETIZERS
- DESSERTS
- SOUPS & SANDWICHES
- HOLIDAY ENTERTAINING
- COOKIES
- VEGETABLES
- MAIN COURSES
- PASTA
- CAKES
- BARBECUES
- DINNERS OF THE WORLD
- LUNCHES
- PIES
- LIGHT RECIPES
- MICROWAVE COOKING
- PRESERVES
- LIGHT CASSEROLES
- CHICKEN, ETC.
- KIDS COOKING
- FISH & SEAFOOD
- BREADS (September '96)

PINT SIZE BOOKS
English

- FINGER FOOD
- PARTY PLANNING
- BUFFETS
- BAKING DELIGHTS
- CHOCOLATE

JEAN PARÉ LIVRES DE CUISINE
French

- 150 DÉLICIEUX CARRÉS
- LES CASSEROLES
- MUFFINS ET PLUS
- LES DÎNERS
- LES BARBECUES
- LES TARTES
- DÉLICES DES FÊTES
- RECETTES LÉGÈRES
- LES SALADES
- LA CUISSON AU MICRO-ONDES
- LES PÂTES
- LES CONSERVES
- LES CASSEROLES LÉGÈRES
- POULET, ETC.
- LA CUISINE POUR LES ENFANTS
- POISSONS ET FRUITS DE MER
- LES PAINS (septembre '96)

table of Contents

Jean Paré grew up understanding that the combination of family, friends and home cooking is the essence of a good life. From her mother she learned to appreciate good cooking, while her father praised even her earliest attempts. When she left home she took with her many acquired family recipes, her love of cooking and her intriguing desire to read recipe books like novels!

In 1963, when her four children had all reached school age, Jean volunteered to cater to the 50th anniversary of the Vermilion School of Agriculture, now Lakeland College. Working out of her home, Jean prepared a dinner for over 1000 people which launched a flourishing catering operation that continued for over eighteen years. During that time she was provided with countless opportunities to test new ideas with immediate feedback—resulting in empty plates and contented customers! Whether preparing cocktail sandwiches for a house party or serving a hot meal for 1500 people, Jean Paré earned a reputation for good food, courteous service and reasonable prices.

"Why don't you write a cookbook?" Time and again, as requests for her recipes mounted, Jean was asked that question. Jean's response was to team up with her son, Grant Lovig, in the fall of 1980 to form Company's Coming Publishing Limited. April 14, 1981, marked the debut of "150 DELICIOUS SQUARES", the first Company's Coming cookbook in what soon would become Canada's most popular cookbook series. By 1995, sales had surpassed ten million cookbooks.

Jean Paré's operation has grown from the early days of working out of a spare bedroom in her home to operating a large and fully equipped test kitchen in Vermilion, Alberta, near the home she and her husband Larry built. Full-time staff has grown steadily to include marketing personnel located in major cities across Canada plus selected U.S. markets. Home Office is located in Edmonton, Alberta where distribution, accounting and administration functions are headquartered in the company's own 20,000 square foot facility. Growth continues with the recent addition of the Recipe Factory, a 2700 square foot test kitchen and photography studio located in Edmonton.

Company's Coming cookbooks are now distributed throughout Canada and the United States plus numerous overseas markets, all under the guidance of another family member, Jean's daughter, Gail Lovig. The series is published in English and French, plus a Spanish language edition is available in Mexico. A recent addition to the family is the smaller, more specialized series called Pint Size Books. Recipes found in these books continue in the familiar and trusted Company's Coming style. Other new formats are planned for release in future.

Jean Paré's approach to cooking has always called for quick and easy recipes using everyday ingredients. She continues to gain new supporters by adhering to what she calls "the golden rule of cooking": never share a recipe you wouldn't use yourself. It's an approach that works—*ten million times over!*

Foreword

Cooking and serving fish and seafood is a pleasurable change as there are so many varieties to choose from and methods of preparation. All recipes can be frozen, except for salads, vegetable and fruit toppings and where otherwise stated.

It makes good nutritional sense to include fish in your diet. Fish is an excellent source of protein, vitamins and minerals. It is generally low in fat and contains omega-3 polyunsaturated fatty acids which have shown to be helpful in reducing the risks of heart disease. The amount of fat varies considerably between different types of fish. Check the Nutrition Guide which follows. Not only can you make good choices for yourself but you can also substitute different varieties of fish within a group as suggested on the Fish Substitution Chart, page 9.

Fresh dressed fish will appear moist and firm with bones firmly attached. Steaks or fillets are best purchased with no sign of drying out or separating of the meat. If fish does not smell clean and fresh — don't buy it. Frozen fish should be solid with no sign of discoloration, freezer burn, or frost crystals on the fish. When defrosted it will compare favorably with fresh fish. To store fresh fish, double-wrap with plastic, forcing out all air, then wrap tightly with aluminum foil. Fresh fish or thawed frozen fish is best cooked within two days.

There are numerous ways to prepare fish and seafood. For those conscious of cholesterol and calorie intake, baking, broiling, poaching or steaming are the best choices. Be careful not to overcook as fish will be tough and dry. Fish is ready to eat when it flakes with a fork. As a general guide, cook fish ten minutes per inch (2.5 cm) at the thickest part. If it is frozen, allow twenty minutes per inch (2.5 cm). Uncooked fish or shellfish has a translucent look, whereas cooked fish is opaque. When cooking shellfish in the shell such as oysters, clams and mussels, check them prior to cooking by tapping the open shells with a spoon or knife. If they don't close, discard. After cooking, eat only the shellfish that have opened. Shucked oysters are cooked when their edges curl.

Sauces, herbs, lemons and limes are wonderful accompaniments to fish. Colorful vegetables and salads will complement any fish or seafood main course. Try Oven Crisp Fish or Captain's Pie for a unique yet satisfying meal. Tasty but with a lighter fish flavor, Crab Soup or Creamy Turbot Soup are both really special. Polynesian Shrimp and Salmon Stuffed Mushrooms are sure to be favorites with family or the next time company's coming. Get hooked on the simple approach to serving fish and seafood.

Jean Paré

COOKING METHODS

Bake: Whole fish, chunks, steaks or fillets can be cooked in the oven. Measure the thickest part of the fish and allow 10 minutes of cooking time per inch (2.5 cm). Cook in a preheated 450°F (230°C) oven. If fish is wrapped in foil, allow an extra 5 to 8 minutes per inch (2.5 cm) of thickness. Frozen fish will take twice as long. To bake uncovered, brush with your choice of melted fat, season fish, or cover with sauce.

Broil: Grease broiler pan. Arrange fish on pan. Brush with melted butter or cooking oil. Broil about 4 inches (10 cm) from heat. If fish is frozen, broil about 8 inches (20 cm) from heat. Turn to brown other side. Season after turning. Allow 10 minutes total time per inch (2.5 cm) of thickness. Allow 20 minutes per inch (2.5 cm) if frozen. Thin fillets can be placed on pan, seasoned and cooked without turning.

Deep-fry: Coat fish in seasoned batter. Pieces should be similar in size. Use fresh or thawed fish. Fry at 375°F to 400°F (190°C to 205°C). Fish will cook quickly, in 1 to 3 minutes depending on thickness. Drain on absorbent paper.

Dry Poach: Wrap fish in foil using double folds to seal. Simmer in water allowing 10 minutes per inch (2.5 cm) of thickness. Allow 20 minutes per inch (2.5 cm) of thickness for frozen fish.

Fry/Grill: This is one of the most popular methods of cooking fish steaks, fillets and small whole fish. It can be fried in butter or hard margarine, or dipped in flour, beaten egg and fried; or it can be dipped in beaten egg then bread crumbs and fried. Allow 10 minutes per inch (2.5 cm) of thickness. Sprinkle with salt and pepper or seasoned bread crumbs.

Poach: Cover fish with water, milk or a Court Bouillon in saucepan. A Court Bouillon is a liquid consisting of water and either wine or lemon juice or vinegar, seasoned with herbs and spices.Cover saucepan. Simmer gently about 5 minutes until fish flakes easily with a fork.

Steam: Place fish in top of steamer with boiling water below. Using cheesecloth around fish makes it easier to remove when cooked. Allow 8 to 10 minutes (20 minutes for frozen) per inch (2.5 cm) of thickness. Cover saucepan. Cook over rapidly boiling water. Do not let water touch fish.

Microwave: Fish should be of even thickness. Thin tips can be folded under. For moist heat, cover with vented plastic wrap. If using coating, cover with paper towel. Fish cooked in the microwave retains moisture well.

FISH SUBSTITUTION CHART

This chart is intended as a guide to help when you want to substitute one fish for another in a recipe. Delicate and medium textured fish can be interchanged with minimal difference. You might choose to substitute from an entirely different flavor grouping depending on personal preference.

Delicate Texture

• MILD FLAVOR •

Black Cod	Flounder	Lingcod
Orange Roughy	Pacific Cod	Sole

• MEDIUM FLAVOR •

Catfish	Pink Salmon	Plaice

Medium Texture

• MILD FLAVOR •

Grouper	Haddock	Halibut
	Snapper	

• MEDIUM FLAVOR •

Chum Salmon	Mahi Mahi	Ocean Perch
Perch	Pickerel	Pollock
Rockfish	Sea Bass	Trout

• FULL FLAVOR •

Atlantic Salmon	Boston Bluefish	Chinook Salmon
Coho Salmon	Fresh Water Carp	King Salmon
Mackerel	Sockeye Salmon	

Firm Texture

• MILD FLAVOR •

Monkfish	Shad	Turbot

• MEDIUM FLAVOR •

Jackfish	Pike	Walleye

• FULL FLAVOR •

Shark	Swordfish	Tuna

NUTRITION GUIDE

Nutrition information for a 3 oz. (85 g) edible portion
of broiled, baked, steamed or poached fish.

FRESH AND SALTWATER FISH	ENERGY Calories (kJ)		CHOLESTEROL (mg)	SODIUM (mg)	FAT (g)	PROTEIN (mg)
Arctic Charr	173	(724)	29	55	8.8	22.0
Boston Bluefish	135	(565)	64	64	4.6	21.8
Carp, Fresh Water	138	(577)	72	54	6.1	19.4
Catfish	127	(531)	63	69	4.6	19.8
Cod - Black	89	(372)	47	66	0.7	19.4
- Pacific	89	(372)	40	77	0.7	19.5
Finnan Haddie	95	(397)	63	74	0.8	20.6
Flounder	99	(414)	58	89	1.3	20.5
Grouper	100	(418)	40	45	1.1	21.1
Haddock	95	(397)	63	74	0.8	20.6
Halibut	119	(498)	35	59	2.5	22.7
Jackfish	96	(401)	43	42	0.7	21.0
Lingcod	93	(389)	57	64	1.2	19.2
Mackerel	171	(711)	51	94	8.6	21.9
Mahi Mahi	92	(385)	79	96	0.8	20.1
Monkfish	82	(343)	27	20	1.7	15.8
Orange Roughy	75	(313)	22	69	0.8	16.0
Perch - Ocean	103	(431)	46	82	1.8	20.3
- Yellow	99	(414)	98	67	1.0	21.0
Pickerel	100	(418)	94	56	0.9	20.9
Pike	101	(422)	94	56	1.3	20.9
Plaice	99	(414)	58	89	1.3	20.5
Pollock	100	(418)	77	94	1.1	21.2
Rockfish	103	(431)	38	65	1.7	20.4
Salmon- Atlantic	155	(648)	60	48	6.9	21.6
- Chinook	196	(820)	72	51	11.4	21.9
- Chum	131	(548)	81	54	4.1	22.0
- Coho	157	(657)	42	50	6.4	23.3
- Keta	131	(548)	81	54	4.1	22.0
- King	196	(820)	72	51	11.4	21.9
- Pink	127	(531)	57	73	3.8	21.7
- Sockeye	183	(766)	74	56	9.3	23.2
- Canned in water w/ salt	116	(485)	20	398	6.3	13.8
- Canned in water w/o salt	116	(485)	20	64	6.3	13.8
Sea Bass - Black	101	(422)	74	74	1.3	20.9
- Striped	106	(443)	87	75	2.5	19.3
Shad	214	(895)	82	56	15.0	18.5
Shark	141	(590)	55	86	4.9	22.8
Snapper	109	(456)	40	48	1.5	22.4
Sole	99	(414)	58	89	1.3	20.5
Swordfish	132	(552)	43	98	4.4	21.6
Trout - Lake	129	(539)	62	29	3.7	22.4
- Ocean	162	(678)	63	57	7.2	22.6
Tuna - Fresh	118	(493)	49	40	1.0	25.5
- Albacore canned in water w/ salt	111	(464)	35	333	2.1	21.7
- Albacore canned in water w/o salt	111	(464)	35	43	2.1	21.7
- Albacore canned in oil w/ salt	158	(661)	26	336	6.9	22.6
- Albacore canned in oil w/o salt	158	(661)	26	43	6.9	22.6
Turbot	104	(435)	52	163	3.2	17.5
Walleye (Yellow)	90	(376)	63	95	1.2	18.6
Whitefish	146	(611)	65	56	6.4	20.8

NUTRITION GUIDE

Nutrition information for a 3 oz. (85 g) edible portion
of boiled, broiled or steamed shellfish

SHELLFISH	ENERGY Calories (kJ)		CHOLESTEROL (mg)	SODIUM (mg)	FAT (g)	PROTEIN (mg)
Clams	126	(527)	57	95	1.7	21.7
Crabmeat	67	(280)	47	306	0.8	12.8
Lobster	93	(389)	61	64	1.2	19.2
Mussels	147	(615)	48	313	4.2	20.2
Oysters	117	(489)	93	190	3.9	12.0
Scallops	96	(401)	36	176	0.8	18.4
Shrimp	84	(351)	166	190	0.9	17.8

How Much Fish To Allow Per Person

DRAWN FISH: Entrails and scales are removed. Allow 1 pound (454 g) per person.

PAN-DRESSED: Entrails, scales and fins are removed. Head and tail are cut off or left on depending on species. Allow ½ pound (225 g) per person.

CHUNKS: Dressed fish is cut into large chunks, part of backbone attached. Allow ½ pound (225 g) per person.

STEAKS: Dressed fish is cut crosswise into steaks. Allow ⅓ to ½ pound (150 to 225 g) per person.

FILLETS: Sides of fish are cut from bones. Allow ⅓ pound (150 g) per person.

SHELLFISH

Clams With Shell: about 20 per person.

Mussels With Shell: about 1½ pounds (675 g) per person.

Oysters With Shell: about 10 per person.

Shelled Crab, Lobster, Oysters, Scallops Or Shrimp: about ⅓ to ½ pound (150 to 225 g) per person.

SHRIMP TURNOVERS

Just the right seasoning in these little golden appetizers. They will disappear quickly.

CREAM CHEESE PASTRY		
Butter or margarine, softened	1 cup	250 mL
Cream cheese, softened	8 oz.	250 g
All-purpose flour	2 cups	500 mL

FILLING		
Tiny cooked shrimp (or 1 can 4 oz., 113 g, rinsed and drained), mashed	1 cup	250 mL
Salad dressing (or mayonnaise)	¼ cup	60 mL
Finely chopped green onions	⅓ cup	75 mL
Lemon juice, fresh or bottled	2 tsp.	10 mL
Prepared mustard	2 tsp.	10 mL

Cream Cheese Pastry: Beat butter and cream cheese together in bowl until smooth.

Add flour. Work in until you can form a ball. Chill in covered bowl for at least 1 hour or overnight.

Filling: Mix all ingredients well. Roll ½ pastry. Cut into 3 inch (7.5 cm) rounds. Place 1 teaspoon (5 mL) filling in center of each round. Dampen half of outer edge with water. Fold over. Press edges together with floured fork or with fingers. Repeat with second ½ of pastry. Arrange on ungreased baking sheet. Cut small slits in each top. Bake in 450°F (230°C) oven for about 10 minutes until golden. Makes about 4 dozen tasty treats.

Pictured on page 17.

Paré Pointer

She was going to go to the end of the line but there was someone there already.

CLAM DIP

Mild in flavor. This recipe could be increased and served in a hollowed out round bread loaf.

Cream cheese, softened	4 oz.	125 g
Canned minced clams, drained	5 oz.	140 g
Lemon juice, fresh or bottled	1 tsp.	5 mL
Garlic powder	¼ tsp.	1 mL
Onion salt	½ tsp.	2 mL
Worcestershire sauce	½ tsp.	2 mL
Milk	2 tbsp.	30 mL
Assorted raw vegetables		

Mix all ingredients well, adding enough milk to make dipping consistency. Chill. Serve with raw vegetables and/or crackers. Makes a generous 1 cup (250 mL).

CLAM CANAPÉS: Pile onto crackers, melba toast or bread rounds. Sprinkle with paprika. Broil until bubbly hot.

CRAB SPREAD

Warm white in color. This is a winner every time!

Unflavored gelatin	1 x ¼ oz.	1 x 7 g
Water	¼ cup	60 mL
Condensed cream of mushroom soup	10 oz.	284 mL
Cream cheese, cut up	8 oz.	250 g
Chopped chives	1 tsp.	5 mL
Onion powder	¼ tsp.	1 mL
Celery salt	⅛ tsp.	0.5 mL
Salad dressing (or mayonnaise)	2 tbsp.	30 mL
Canned crabmeat, drained, membrane removed	4.2 oz.	120 g
Frilly lettuce		
Assorted crackers		

Sprinkle gelatin over water in small cup. Let stand.

Heat next 5 ingredients in saucepan, stirring often. When mixture is melted and hot, stir in gelatin mixture to dissolve. Remove from heat.

Add salad dressing and crabmeat. Stir. Pour into 3 cup (750 mL) ring mold. Chill. Cover serving plate with frilly lettuce. Unmold Crab Spread. Serve with crackers. Best not to freeze. Makes 3 cups (750 mL).

Pictured on page 17.

TUNA BUTTER SPREAD

It can't get much easier than this. Smooth and tasty. Easy to increase the recipe. A little goes a long way.

Canned tuna, oil packed, drained (or add a bit of cooking oil to water packed)	¼ cup	60 mL
Butter or hard margarine, softened	½ cup	125 mL
Assorted crackers		

Run tuna and butter through blender. This will take about 10 seconds. Shape in a mound or pack into small bowl. Chill. Serve with a variety of crackers. Makes ⅔ cup (150 mL).

BEER BATTERED SEAFOOD

A combination deep-fried fish platter is always the first tray to be emptied.

All-purpose flour	1½ cups	375 mL
Salt	1 tbsp.	15 mL
Pepper	1 tbsp.	15 mL
Cayenne pepper, just a pinch		
Beer (1 can 12 oz., 355 mL)	1½ cups	375 mL
Shrimp, oysters, onion rings, cubed fish fillets, scallops	2 lbs.	900 g
All-purpose flour	1 cup	250 mL
Fine dry bread crumbs	1 cup	250 mL
Fat for deep-frying		

Stir first 5 ingredients together in small bowl.

Dip individual pieces of fish or seafood into second amount of flour, then into batter.

Coat with bread crumbs.

Drop a few pieces into hot 400°F (205°C) fat. Remove with slotted spoon when brown. May also be cooked without coating in bread crumbs. Will be deeper brown with crumbs. Coats about 2 pounds (900 g) of fish/seafood.

What a winner! Large scallops may also be prepared this way.

Large egg	1	1
Water	2 tbsp.	30 mL
Fine dry bread crumbs	1 cup	250 mL
Salt	½ tsp.	2 mL
Pepper	¼ tsp.	1 mL
Paprika	1 tsp.	5 mL
Cayenne pepper, just a pinch		
Small scallops	1 lb.	454 g
Butter or hard margarine, melted	¼ cup	60 mL

Beat egg and water in small bowl with fork.

In another bowl stir next 5 ingredients to mix.

Pierce scallop with toothpick and dip in crumb mixture, then in egg mixture, then in crumb mixture again. Put coated scallops on greased baking sheet with sides. Let stand 30 minutes.

Dab melted butter over scallops with pastry brush. Bake, uncovered, in 450°F (230°C) oven for about 15 minutes until browned. Serve with Seafood Sauce, page 139, or Tartar Sauce, page 140, for dipping. Makes about 9 dozen tiny appetizers.

Pictured on page 17.

Paré Pointer

He may be penniless but the czar of Russia was Nicholas.

NUTTY CRAB BALL

Cream cheese is the base for this instead of Cheddar. It has an orangy color and good flavor with a bit of a bite.

Cream cheese, softened	8 oz.	250 g
Ketchup	1 tbsp.	15 mL
Lemon juice, fresh or bottled	2 tsp.	5 mL
Pimiento-stuffed olives, finely chopped	6	6
Worcestershire sauce	1/2 tsp.	2 mL
Onion powder	1 tsp.	5 mL
Canned crabmeat, drained, membrane removed, flaked	4.2 oz.	120 g
Chopped pecans	1/2 cup	125 mL
Assorted crackers		

Beat or mash first 7 ingredients together in bowl. Chill for about 1 hour until it is firm enough to shape into a ball.

Roll in chopped pecans. Chill. May be made up ahead of time, wrapped snugly in 2 layers of plastic wrap, then foil, and frozen. Best served at room temperature. Serve with assorted crackers. Makes 1 ball, about 3 1/2 inches (9 cm) in diameter.

Pictured on page 17.

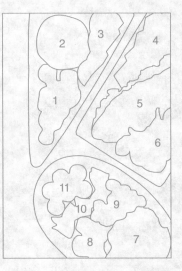

Dishes Courtesy Of:
Artifacts

Stained Glass Courtesy Of:
Winter Art Glass

Put these on crackers or toast squares for a tasty appetizer, or use right from the pan as a main course.

Large eggs	2	2
Canned tuna, drained and flaked	6½ oz.	184 g
Chopped chives	1 tsp.	5 mL
Salt	⅛ tsp.	0.5 mL
Crackers, or toast squares	18	18

Beat eggs with fork in bowl. Add next 3 ingredients. Mix well.

Drop teaspoonfuls into medium-hot greased frying pan. Press down lightly to flatten into a patty. Brown both sides.

Place each patty on cracker or toast square. Serve hot. Patties can be made ahead and reheated on cracker or toast square, on ungreased baking sheet, in 425°F (220°C) oven for about 5 minutes until hot. Makes 18 small patties.

SALMON STUFFED MUSHROOMS

Crunchy with a good salmon flavor. Filling will freeze.

Large mushrooms	12	12
Fresh salmon, cooked (or ½ can 7½ oz., 213 g, drained)	½ cup	125 mL
Chopped mushroom stems		
Dry bread crumbs	¼ cup	60 mL
Chopped chives	1 tbsp.	15 mL
Water	¼ cup	60 mL
Seasoned salt	½ tsp.	2 mL
Grated Parmesan cheese, sprinkle		

Remove stems from mushrooms. Chop stems.

Remove skin and round bones from salmon. Flake.

Mix salmon with next 5 ingredients. Stuff mushroom caps.

Sprinkle with cheese or dip tops into cheese. Arrange on baking sheet. Bake in 425°F (220°C) oven for about 10 minutes. Makes 1 cup (250 mL) filling which will stuff 12 to 18 mushrooms, depending on size.

Pictured on page 17.

CRAB STUFFED PEAS

Green pods stuffed with a light colored filling. Filling will freeze.

Cream cheese, softened	4 oz.	125 g
Lemon juice, fresh or bottled	1 tsp.	5 mL
Sherry (or alcohol-free sherry)	1 tbsp.	15 mL
Prepared mustard	½ tsp.	2 mL
Salad dressing (or mayonnaise)	2 tbsp.	30 mL
Chopped chives	1½ tbsp.	25 mL
Canned crabmeat, drained, membrane removed	4.2 oz.	120 g
Snow peas, frozen, thawed (see Note)	6 oz.	170 g

Mash first 6 ingredients in shallow bowl.

Add crabmeat. Mix well.

Slit peas on top side which is the least curved side. Stuff pods using about 1 tsp. (5 mL) each. Cover and chill for 2 hours before serving. Makes a generous 1 cup (250 mL).

Note: If using fresh pods, cover with boiling water. Let stand 10 minutes. Drain. Rinse with cold water. Drain.

CRAB STUFFED CHERRY TOMATOES: Cut tops off tomatoes. Scoop out centers with small spoon. Fill with crab mixture.

Pictured on page 17.

CRAB ROUNDS

These can be made up ahead to broil when needed. An extra bonus is that they can be broiled from the frozen state.

Butter or hard margarine, softened	½ cup	125 mL
Process cheese spread, softened	½ cup	125 mL
Salad dressing (or mayonnaise)	1 tbsp.	15 mL
Seasoned salt	½ tsp.	2 mL
Chopped chives	2 tsp.	10 mL
Crabmeat (or 1 can 4.2 oz., 120 g, drained), membrane removed	1 cup	250 mL
Dark bread slices		

(continued on next page)

Beat first 5 ingredients in small mixing bowl until smooth.

Stir in crabmeat.

Cut bread into rounds with 1½ inch (4 cm) or 1¾ inch (4.5 cm) biscuit cutter. Spread with crabmeat mixture. Broil until bubbly hot. Makes 1⅓ cups (325 mL) filling.

Pictured on page 17.

BROILED CRABWICHES: Spread thick bread slices or bun halves with filling. Broil until bubbly.

SALMON PATÉ

So smooth with a creamy palate-pleasing taste. It has a zip but yet it's mild.

Butter or hard margarine	**½ cup**	**125 mL**
Canned salmon (red, such as sockeye, is best for color), drained	**7½ oz.**	**213 g**
Lemon juice, fresh or bottled	**2 tsp.**	**10 mL**
Dill weed	**⅛ tsp.**	**0.5 mL**
Chopped chives	**1 tbsp.**	**15 mL**
Salad dressing (or mayonnaise)	**2 tbsp.**	**30 mL**
Prepared mustard	**½ tsp.**	**2 mL**
Salt	**⅛ tsp.**	**0.5 mL**
Cream cheese, cut up	**4 oz.**	**125 g**

Assorted crackers or dark bread

Melt butter in saucepan. Pour into blender.

Remove skin and round bones from salmon. Add salmon and next 7 ingredients to blender. Process until smooth. Pour into bowl. Chill.

Serve with crackers or small dark squares of bread. Makes a generous 1½ cups (375 mL).

Paré Pointer

It used to be when a man talked about retiring he meant he was going to bed.

TRIANGLE APPETIZERS

These golden little bundles contain a mild tasty filling.

FILLING

Grated medium Cheddar cheese	1 cup	250 mL
Canned crabmeat, drained, membrane removed	4.2 oz.	120 g
Parsley flakes	1 tsp.	5 mL
Chopped green onion	1 tbsp.	15 mL
Salad dressing (or mayonnaise)	3 tbsp.	50 mL
Tubes of refrigerator crescent rolls	2	2

COATING

Egg white (large)	1	1
Sesame seeds	1 tbsp.	15 mL

Filling: Combine first 5 ingredients in bowl. Mix well.

Separate crescent rolls. Lay all the rolls out flat. Divide filling among them, using about 1 tbsp. (15 mL) for each. Place filling in center. Gather 2 long end corners together then pull up 3rd corner. Pinch together. Repeat for each roll.

Coating: Beat egg white with fork in small bowl. Brush each roll with egg white. Sprinkle with sesame seeds. Arrange on greased baking sheet. Bake in 350°F (175°C) oven for 15 to 18 minutes until browned. Serve hot. Cold leftovers are good too. Makes 16.

Pictured on page 17.

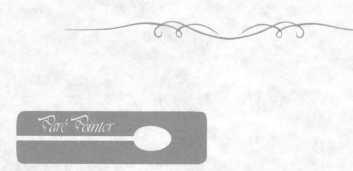

Paré Pointer

Arthritis is twinges in the hinges.

CRAB CANAPÉS

These are so-o-o good! You will need to make the whole recipe even though it makes lots. Lots is what you'll need.

Process cheese spread containing aged Cheddar (such as Ingersoll)	1 cup	250 mL
Butter or hard margarine, softened	½ cup	125 mL
Salad dressing (or mayonnaise)	1½ tbsp.	25 mL
Garlic salt	1 tsp.	5 mL
Canned crabmeat, drained, membrane removed	4.2 oz.	120 g
English muffins	8	8

Beat cheese, butter, salad dressing, garlic salt and crabmeat together in bowl until mixed and smooth.

Split muffins. Spread each half with 2 tbsp. (30 mL) crab mixture. Arrange on broiling tray. Broil until lightly browned. Cut each muffin half into 6 pieces. These may be frozen ahead ready to broil, cut and serve. Makes 8 dozen delicious appetizers.

Pictured on page 17.

SHRIMP DIP

The addition of Cheddar cheese makes this colorful. Tastes great with a faint hint of dill.

Finely grated mild Cheddar cheese	1 cup	250 mL
Salad dressing (or mayonnaise)	⅓ cup	75 mL
Sour cream	3 tbsp.	50 mL
Onion flakes	1 tbsp.	15 mL
Lemon juice, fresh or bottled	1 tsp.	5 mL
Paprika	¼ tsp.	1 mL
Dill weed	¼ tsp.	1 mL
Canned broken shrimp, rinsed, drained and mashed	4 oz.	113 g
Milk, if required		

Mix first 7 ingredients in bowl.

Add shrimp. Mash together adding a bit of milk if too stiff for dipping consistency. Makes 1¼ cups (300 mL).

SHRIMP AND ARTICHOKE DIP

A chunky dip or spread. Mild but flavorful.

Cream cheese, softened	4 oz.	125 g
Salad dressing (or mayonnaise)	½ cup	125 mL
Sour cream	½ cup	125 mL
Chopped green onion	¼ cup	60 mL
Salt	½ tsp.	2 mL
Pepper	⅛ tsp.	0.5 mL
Canned artichoke hearts, drained and finely chopped	14 oz.	398 mL
Canned broken shrimp, rinsed and drained (or whole shrimp, chopped)	4 oz.	113 g
Assorted crackers		

Beat cream cheese, salad dressing, sour cream, onion, salt and pepper together.

Add artichoke and shrimp. Stir together.

Serve with crackers as a dip or as a spread. Makes 2¾ cups (675 mL).

Pare Pointer

Should you ever hear dot-dot-croak, dot-dot-croak, you just heard Morris Toad.

A golden top with pimiento, shrimp and mushrooms visible. Good choice.

Elbow macaroni	2 cups	500 mL
Boiling water	3 qts.	3 L
Cooking oil	1 tbsp.	15 mL
Salt	2 tsp.	10 mL
Condensed cream of mushroom soup	2 × 10 oz.	2 × 284 mL
Milk	1 cup	250 mL
Crabmeat (or 1 can 4.2 oz., 120 g, drained), membrane removed	1 cup	250 mL
Small cooked shrimp (or 1 can 4 oz., 113 g, rinsed and drained)	1 cup	250 mL
Canned mushroom pieces, drained	10 oz.	284 mL
Diced pimiento	¼ cup	60 mL
Grated Parmesan cheese	½ cup	125 mL
Garlic salt	1 tsp.	5 mL
Cayenne pepper	⅛ tsp.	0.5 mL
Grated Parmesan cheese	½ cup	125 mL
Butter or hard margarine	2 tbsp.	30 mL

Cook macaroni in boiling water, cooking oil and salt in large uncovered pot for 5 to 7 minutes until tender but firm. Drain. Return macaroni to pot.

Heat and stir soup and milk in saucepan.

Add next 7 ingredients. Stir. Add to macaroni in pot. Stir. Turn into ungreased 3 quart (3 L) casserole.

Sprinkle with remaining cheese. Dot with bits of butter. Bake, uncovered, in 350°F (175°C) oven for about 30 minutes until hot and bubbly. Serves 6 to 8.

Pictured on page 35.

SCALLOP BAKE

This crispy onion-topped dish is a real treat.

Hard margarine (butter browns too fast)	2 tbsp.	30 mL
Chopped onion	¾ cup	175 mL
Chopped fresh mushrooms	2 cups	500 mL
All-purpose flour	2 tbsp.	30 mL
Salt	½ tsp.	2 mL
Pepper	¼ tsp.	1 mL
Milk	1 cup	250 mL
Scallops, quarter large ones	1 lb.	454 g
Canned French fried onions	2¾ oz.	79 g

Melt margarine in frying pan. Add onion. Sauté 3 minutes.

Add mushrooms. Sauté about 5 minutes more.

Mix in flour, salt and pepper. Stir in milk until it boils and thickens.

Add scallops. Stir. Turn into ungreased 2 quart (2 L) casserole. Bake, uncovered, in 350°F (175°C) oven for 30 minutes.

Cover with onions. Bake about 10 minutes more to heat through. Serves 4 to 6.

TUNA STRATA

Tuna sandwiches in an egg and milk sauce. Toasty bread topping. A good choice for lunch.

Bread slices, crusts removed	12	12
Canned tuna, drained and flaked	2 × 6½ oz.	2 × 184 g
Tomato sauce	7½ oz.	213 mL
Granulated sugar	1 tsp.	5 mL
Onion powder	¼ tsp.	1 mL
SAUCE		
Large eggs	4	4
Milk	1½ cups	375 mL
Salt	1 tsp.	5 mL
Pepper	⅛ tsp.	0.5 mL
Chili powder	¼ tsp.	1 mL

(continued on next page)

Arrange 6 bread slices in greased 9 × 13 inch (22 × 33 cm) pan.

Divide tuna among bread slices in pan. Spread to cover each slice.

Mix tomato sauce, sugar and onion powder in small bowl. Spoon over tuna. Cover with 6 remaining bread slices.

Sauce: Beat eggs in mixing bowl until frothy. Add milk, salt, pepper and chili powder. Pour over all. Chill for about 45 minutes. Bake, uncovered, in 350°F (175°C) oven for about 35 minutes until browned. Serves 6.

Pictured on page 35.

SEA CRAB DISH

Mild in flavor. Very attractive with colorful zucchini and tomatoes.

Hard margarine (butter browns too fast)	6 tbsp.	100 mL
Sliced zucchini, with peel	3 cups	750 mL
Chopped onion	1 cup	250 mL
Medium tomatoes	4	4
Granulated sugar	$\frac{1}{2}$ tsp.	2 mL
Salt	$\frac{1}{2}$ tsp.	2 mL
Pepper	$\frac{1}{8}$ tsp.	0.5 mL
Garlic powder	$\frac{1}{4}$ tsp.	1 mL
Grated Swiss cheese	$1\frac{1}{2}$ cups	375 mL
Dry bread crumbs	$\frac{3}{4}$ cup	175 mL
Crabmeat (or 2 × 4.2 oz., 2 × 120 g cans, drained), membrane removed	$\frac{1}{2}$ lb.	250 g

Melt margarine in large frying pan. Add zucchini and onion. Sauté about 5 minutes until tender. You may have to do this in 2 batches.

Cut tomatoes into 4 or 6 wedges each. Using handle of teaspoon, remove seeds as you lightly squeeze each wedge. Dice tomato sections and add to zucchini mixture. Add sugar, salt, pepper and garlic powder. Stir together well.

Add cheese, bread crumbs and crabmeat. Stir. Turn into ungreased 2 quart (2 L) casserole. Bake, uncovered, in 350°F (175°C) oven for 30 to 40 minutes until hot. Serves 6.

Pictured on page 35.

SALMON AMANDINE

A salmon dish full of crunch and flavor.

Hard margarine (butter browns too fast)	2 tbsp.	30 mL
Chopped onion	1½ cups	375 mL
Finely chopped green pepper	¼ cup	60 mL
Canned salmon, drained, juice reserved	2 × 7½ oz.	2 × 213 g
Cooked rice	2 cups	500 mL
Parsley flakes	2 tsp.	10 mL
Condensed cream of mushroom soup	10 oz.	284 mL
Milk	1 cup	250 mL
Coarsely crushed potato chips	2½ cups	625 mL
(about 2 × 2 oz., 2 × 55 g bags)		
Slivered almonds	¾ cup	175 mL

Melt margarine in frying pan. Add onion and green pepper. Sauté until soft.

Remove skin and round bones from salmon. Put salmon with reserved juice in bowl. Flake salmon. Add rice and parsley. Stir lightly. Add onion mixture. Stir lightly.

In another bowl stir soup and milk together well.

Assemble in greased 3 quart (3 L) casserole as follows:

1. ½ crushed potato chips

2. ½ salmon mixture

3. ½ soup mixture

4. ½ salmon mixture

5. ½ soup mixture

6. ½ crushed potato chips

7. All slivered almonds

Bake, uncovered, in 375°F (190°C) oven for about 45 minutes. Serves 6 to 8.

Add salad and/or a vegetable and you have a full meal.

Medium potatoes, peeled and quartered	4	4
Boiling salted water		
Hard margarine (butter browns too fast)	¼ cup	60 mL
Chopped onion	1 cup	250 mL
Chopped green pepper (optional)	¼ cup	60 mL
All-purpose flour	¼ cup	60 mL
Salt	1 tsp.	5 mL
Pepper	¼ tsp.	1 mL
Milk	2 cups	500 mL
Canned salmon, drained	2 × 7½ oz.	2 × 213 g
TOPPING		
Butter or hard margarine	2 tbsp.	30 mL
Dry bread crumbs	½ cup	125 mL
Grated Parmesan cheese	3 tbsp.	50 mL

Cook potatoes in boiling water until tender. Drain. Cool until you can handle them. Slice ½ of potatoes into greased 2 quart (2 L) casserole.

Melt margarine in frying pan. Add onion and green pepper. Sauté slowly until soft.

Mix in flour, salt and pepper. Stir in milk until it boils and thickens. Pour ½ of sauce over potato layer.

Remove skin and round bones from salmon. Flake salmon and arrange over sauce layer. Slice second ½ of potatoes over salmon followed by second ½ of sauce.

Topping: Melt butter in small saucepan. Add bread crumbs and cheese. Stir. Sprinkle over all. Bake, uncovered, in 350°F (175°C) oven for about 30 minutes until heated through. Serves 4 to 6.

DILLED FISH CASSEROLE

Quick to make. Flavored by dill weed and salad dressing. Fish is added raw.

Canned sliced mushrooms, drained	10 oz.	284 mL
Chopped green onion	¼ cup	60 mL
Parsley flakes	½ tsp.	2 mL
Dill weed	½ tsp.	2 mL
Ocean perch or cod fillets	1 lb.	454 g
Sour cream	⅔ cup	150 mL
Salad dressing (or mayonnaise)	⅓ cup	75 mL
All-purpose flour	1½ tbsp.	25 mL
Salt	½ tsp.	2 mL
Pepper	⅛ tsp.	0.5 mL
Paprika	⅛ tsp.	0.5 mL
TOPPING		
Butter or hard margarine	2 tbsp.	30 mL
Dry bread crumbs	½ cup	125 mL

Stir first 4 ingredients together in ungreased 2 quart (2 L) casserole.

Cut fish fillets into serving size pieces. Arrange over mushroom mixture.

Mix next 6 ingredients in small bowl. Spread over fish.

Topping: Melt butter in small saucepan. Stir in bread crumbs. Sprinkle over all. Bake, uncovered, in 375°F (190°C) oven for about 30 minutes until fish flakes. Serves 4.

Pictured on page 35.

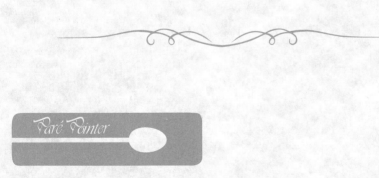

Kelly learned in school that it takes more than one sheep to make a sweater. He didn't even know they could knit.

A chive biscuit topping covers sauced tuna and peas. Just add potatoes, noodles or rice for a complete meal.

Hard margarine (butter browns too fast)	1/4 cup	60 mL
Chopped onion	1/4 cup	60 mL
Chopped green pepper	2 tbsp.	30 mL
All-purpose flour	1/4 cup	60 mL
Salt	1/2 tsp.	2 mL
Pepper	1/8 tsp.	0.5 mL
Milk	1 1/2 cups	375 mL
Cooked peas (or half peas and half other cooked vegetable)	2 cups	500 mL
Canned tuna, drained and flaked	2 × 6 1/2 oz.	2 × 184 g

CHIVE BISCUITS

All-purpose flour	1 cup	250 mL
Baking powder	2 tsp.	10 mL
Chopped chives	1 tbsp.	15 mL
Salt	1/4 tsp.	1 mL
Butter or hard margarine	3 tbsp.	50 mL
Milk	6 tbsp.	100 mL

Melt margarine in saucepan. Add onion and green pepper. Sauté until soft.

Mix in flour, salt and pepper. Stir in milk until it boils and thickens.

And peas and tuna. Stir. Pour into ungreased 2 quart (2 L) casserole.

Chive Biscuits: Measure flour, baking powder, chives and salt into bowl. Cut in butter until mixture is crumbly.

Add milk. Stir to form soft ball. Knead 5 or 6 times on lightly floured surface. Roll or pat to 1/2 inch (12 mm) thick. Cut with fish shaped cookie cutter or in 2 inch (5 cm) rounds. Arrange over casserole. Bake, uncovered, in 425°F (220°C) oven for 20 to 25 minutes until biscuits are risen and browned. Makes 6 servings.

CORN AND SALMON BAKE

Good color and flavor combination.

Canola oil
or
olive
oil

Hard margarine (butter browns too fast)	2 tbsp.	30 mL
Chopped onion	½ cup	125 mL
Chopped celery	¼ cup	60 mL
Canned salmon, juice reserved	7½ oz.	213 g
Milk	1 cup	250 mL
Saltine cracker crumbs	1 cup	250 mL
Canned cream-style corn	14 oz.	398 mL
Large eggs, fork beaten	2	2
Grated medium Cheddar cheese	1 cup	250 mL
TOPPING		
Butter or hard margarine	2 tbsp.	30 mL
Dry bread crumbs	½ cup	125 mL

Melt margarine in frying pan. Add onion and celery. Sauté until soft.

Remove skin and round bones from salmon. Flake salmon. Add salmon with juice and next 5 ingredients to onion and celery. Turn into ungreased 2 quart (2 L) casserole.

Topping: Melt butter in small saucepan. Stir in bread crumbs. Sprinkle over top. Bake, uncovered, in 350°F (175°C) oven for 45 to 55 minutes until an inserted knife comes out clean. Serves 4 to 6.

SALMON BAKE

Asparagus and salmon baked in a creamy sauce.

Canned asparagus pieces, drained	10 oz.	284 mL
Canned salmon, drained	7½ oz.	213 g
Butter or hard margarine	2 tbsp.	30 mL
All-purpose flour	2 tbsp.	30 mL
Salt	½ tsp.	2 mL
Pepper	⅛ tsp.	0.5 mL
Milk	1 cup	250 mL
Paprika	⅛ tsp.	0.5 mL

(continued on next page)

Arrange asparagus in bottom of ungreased 1 quart (1 L) casserole. Remove skin and round bones from salmon. Flake salmon and scatter over top.

Melt butter in saucepan. Mix in flour, salt and pepper. Stir in milk until it boils and thickens. Pour over salmon.

Sprinkle with paprika. Bake, uncovered, in 350°F (175°C) oven for 20 to 30 minutes until heated through. Serves 4.

TUNA ROTINI BAKE

A tasty dish using a convenience sauce. The cheesy topping finishes this quick meal.

Hard margarine (butter browns too fast)	2 tbsp.	30 mL
Chopped onion	½ cup	125 mL
Chopped green pepper	¼ cup	60 mL
Canned tuna, drained and flaked	6½ oz.	184 g
Condensed cream of chicken soup	10 oz.	284 mL
Canned mushroom pieces, drained	10 oz.	284 mL
Grated medium Cheddar cheese	½ cup	125 mL
Rotini pasta	2 cups	500 mL
Boiling water	3 qts.	3 L
Cooking oil	1 tbsp.	15 mL
Salt	2 tsp.	10 mL
Grated medium Cheddar cheese	½ cup	125 mL

Melt margarine in large saucepan. Add onion and green pepper. Sauté until soft.

Add tuna, soup, mushrooms and first amount of cheese. Stir. Set aside.

Cook rotini in boiling water, cooking oil and salt in large uncovered pot for 10 to 12 minutes until tender but firm. Drain. Add to tuna mixture. Stir. Turn into 2 quart (2 L) ungreased casserole. Sprinkle with remaining cheese. Cover. Bake in 350°F (175°C) oven for about 30 minutes until bubbly hot. Serves 4 to 6.

FISH AU GRATIN CASSEROLE

Good for the day's catch. Just add onion, cover with a sauce and bake.

Fish fillets	1½ lbs.	680 g
Salt	½ tsp.	2 mL
Cooking oil	2 tbsp.	30 mL
Chopped onion	1 cup	250 mL
All-purpose flour	3 tbsp.	50 mL
Salt	½ tsp.	2 mL
Pepper	⅛ tsp.	0.5 mL
Milk	1½ cups	375 mL
Grated medium Cheddar cheese	1 cup	250 mL

Lay fish fillets in greased 3 quart (3 L) casserole. Sprinkle with first amount of salt.

Heat cooking oil in frying pan. Add onion. Sauté gently until soft.

Mix flour, salt and pepper into onion. Stir in milk until it boils and thickens. Pour over fish.

Sprinkle with cheese. Bake, uncovered, in 350°F (175°C) oven for 30 to 35 minutes until fish flakes easily. Serves 4 to 6.

Thyme changes everything!

Long grain rice	1 cup	250 mL
Boiling water	2 cups	500 mL
Salt	1 tsp.	5 mL
Cooking oil	1 tbsp.	15 mL
Chopped onion	1½ cups	375 mL
Ground thyme	¼ tsp.	1 mL
Halibut or cod fillets	1-1½ lbs.	454-680 g
Tomato sauce	7½ oz.	213 g
Lemon juice, fresh or bottled	1 tbsp.	15 mL
Granulated sugar	½ tsp.	2 mL
Salt	¼ tsp.	1 mL
Pepper	¼ tsp.	1 mL

TOPPING

Grated medium Cheddar cheese	1 cup	250 mL
Dry bread crumbs	¼ cup	60 mL

Add rice to salted boiling water in saucepan. Cover. Reduce heat and simmer for about 15 minutes until tender and water is absorbed.

Heat cooking oil in frying pan. Add onion. Sauté until clear and soft. Stir into rice.

Add thyme to rice mixture. Stir. Turn into ungreased 2 quart (2 L) casserole.

Cut fish into serving size pieces. Lay pieces over rice mixture.

Stir next 5 ingredients together in small bowl. Spoon over fish, spreading evenly.

Topping: Combine cheese and bread crumbs in small bowl. Sprinkle over top. Bake, uncovered, in 350°F (175°C) oven for about 35 minutes until fish flakes and cheese starts to brown. Serves 4 to 6.

SALMON PASTA

A full meal dish with cheese and mushrooms added. The asparagus dresses it up.

Hard margarine (butter browns too fast)	¼ cup	60 mL
Chopped onion	½ cup	125 mL
All-purpose flour	¼ cup	60 mL
Salt	1 tsp.	5 mL
Paprika	¼ tsp.	1 mL
Dry mustard powder	¼ tsp.	1 mL
Milk	3 cups	750 mL
Canned salmon, drained	2 x 7½ oz.	2 x 213 g
Worcestershire sauce	1 tsp.	5 mL
Grated medium Cheddar cheese	½ cup	125 mL
Canned sliced mushrooms, drained	10 oz.	284 mL
Chopped olives (optional, but good)	½ cup	125 mL
Large pasta shells (not jumbo)	8 oz.	250 g
Boiling water	3 qts.	3 L
Cooking oil	1 tbsp.	15 mL
Salt	2 tsp.	10 mL
Canned asparagus pieces (or 1 can 14 oz., 398 mL, green beans), drained	10 oz.	284 mL

TOPPING

Butter or hard margarine	2 tbsp.	30 mL
Dry bread crumbs	½ cup	125 mL
Grated medium Cheddar cheese	¼ cup	60 mL

Melt margarine in large saucepan. Add onion. Sauté until soft.

Mix in flour, salt, paprika and mustard powder. Stir in milk until it boils and thickens.

Remove skin and round bones from salmon. Flake salmon and add with next 4 ingredients to saucepan. Stir. Set aside.

Cook shells in boiling water, cooking oil and salt in large uncovered pot for about 13 minutes until tender but firm. Drain. Return shells to pot. Add salmon mixture. Stir. Pour into ungreased 3 quart (3 L) casserole.

Arrange asparagus over top.

Topping: Melt butter in small saucepan. Stir in bread crumbs and cheese. Sprinkle over asparagus. Bake, uncovered, in 350°F (175°C) oven for about 30 minutes until browned and hot. Serves 6.

Pictured on page 35.

MIXED SEAFOOD CASSEROLE

A fabulous dish to spoon over rice. So tasty. So different.

MIXED SEAFOOD

A combination of scallops, crab, shrimp, cubed cod, cubed sole	2 lbs.	900 g
Boiling water	2 cups	500 mL
Butter or hard margarine	6 tbsp.	100 mL
Sliced fresh mushrooms	1 cup	250 mL
All-purpose flour	1/3 cup	75 mL
Chicken bouillon powder	1 tbsp.	15 mL
Reserved stock		
Evaporated skim milk (or light cream)	1 cup	250 mL
Grated medium Cheddar cheese	1 cup	250 mL
Worcestershire sauce	1/8 tsp.	0.5 mL
Cayenne pepper, just a pinch		
Croutons	3 cups	750 mL

Mixed Seafood: Combine seafood. Add to boiling water in saucepan. Simmer for about 5 minutes until fish flakes when tested with fork, scallops are opaque and shrimp pinkish and curled. Drain and reserve fish stock.

Melt butter in frying pan. Add mushrooms. Sauté until soft.

Mix in flour and bouillon powder. Stir in reserved stock until it boils and thickens.

Add milk, cheese, Worcestershire sauce and cayenne. Stir to melt cheese. Add assorted seafood. Turn into ungreased 3 quart (3 L) casserole.

Pour croutons over top. Mix with spoon to distribute throughout. Bake, uncovered, in 375°F (190°C) oven for 25 to 30 minutes until golden. Serve over rice. Serves 6 to 8.

Paré Pointer

A bug that usually sleeps in a dish is a bowl-weevil.

SCALLOPED OYSTERS

A double duty dish. Have Scalloped Oysters or make into Oyster Soup simply by adding more milk. Do not freeze.

Soda crackers	16	16
Small oysters (Atlantic are smaller)	2 cups	500 mL
Salt, sprinkle		
Pepper, sprinkle		
Butter or hard margarine	6 tbsp.	100 mL
Homogenized milk, for richness	3 cups	750 mL

Break up 4 crackers into greased 2 quart (2 L) casserole. Spoon ⅓ oysters over top. Sprinkle with salt and pepper. Dot with ⅓ butter. Repeat 2 more times. Break remaining 4 crackers over top.

Pour milk over all. Cover. Refrigerate for several hours or overnight to allow milk to be absorbed by crackers. Gently fold top oysters down and bring bottom oysters up. Bake, uncovered, in 350°F (175°C) oven for about 45 minutes until it bubbles around the edges. Serves 4.

OYSTER SOUP: No need to layer ingredients or to refrigerate before cooking. Add 1 cup (250 mL) milk to above recipe. Put all ingredients into saucepan and simmer until edges of oysters curl. Makes about 4¾ cups (1.2 L).

CHILI CRAB

No pre-cooking. Rice is added raw. Extra chili powder may be added if desired.

Long grain rice, uncooked	1 cup	250 mL
Sliced fresh mushrooms	1 cup	250 mL
Medium green pepper, seeded and very finely chopped (optional)	1	1
Onion flakes	¼ cup	60 mL
Crabmeat (or 2 × 4.2 oz., 2 × 120 g cans, drained), membrane removed	½ lb.	250 g
Salad dressing (or mayonnaise)	⅔ cup	150 mL
Milk	1 cup	250 mL
Tomato sauce	7½ oz.	213 g
Chili powder	2 tsp.	10 mL
Salt	½ tsp.	2 mL
Pepper	⅛ tsp.	0.5 mL

(continued on next page)

Combine first 5 ingredients in ungreased 2 quart (2 L) casserole. Stir to distribute evenly.

Mix next 6 ingredients in bowl. Pour into casserole. Stir. Cover. Bake in 350°F (175°C) oven for 1 hour. Serves 4 to 6.

QUICKBREAD MUFFINS

A perfect meal-type muffin. These are not sweet.

Large egg	1	1
Milk	1 cup	250 mL
Cooking oil	¼ cup	60 mL
All-purpose flour	2 cups	500 mL
Granulated sugar	1½ tbsp.	25 mL
Baking powder	4 tsp.	20 mL
Salt	¾ tsp.	4 mL

Beat egg in bowl until frothy. Add milk and cooking oil. Mix.

In separate bowl, stir flour, sugar, baking powder and salt. Add to egg mixture. Stir with a spoon until just moistened. Fill greased muffin cups ¾ full. Bake in 400°F (205°C) oven for about 20 minutes until an inserted wooden pick comes out clean. Let stand for about 5 minutes before removing from pan to cool. Makes 12.

LOCKER BISCUITS

Davey Jones must have had these in his locker on the ocean floor. Baked in tiny tart tins they rise high to the occasion.

Biscuit mix	3 cups	750 mL
Granulated sugar	3 tbsp.	50 mL
Cold beer	1¼ cups	300 mL

Mix all 3 ingredients. Dough will be very soft. Fill greased tiny tart tins to the top. Bake in 450°F (230°C) oven for 12 to 15 minutes until risen and browned. Makes 2½ dozen.

Pictured on page 35.

GRILLED BREAD

Grilling allows for easy preparation of a few slices or several.

Butter or hard margarine, softened	½ cup	125 mL
Salad dressing (or mayonnaise)	¼ cup	60 mL
Grated Parmesan cheese	⅓ cup	75 mL
Parsley flakes	½ tsp.	2 mL
Onion powder	¼ tsp.	1 mL
French bread, sliced 1 inch (2.5 cm) thick		

Mix first 5 ingredients in small bowl.

Spread both sides of each bread slice with butter mixture. Brown both sides in greased medium-hot frying pan. Makes 1 loaf.

CUCUMBER VEGGIE

A unique vegetable. The green color goes so well with fish. Do not freeze.

Large unpeeled cucumbers, halved lengthwise, seeds removed, sliced ½ inch (12 mm) thick	3	3
Boiling water	2 cups	500 mL
Salt	½ tsp.	2 mL
Butter or hard margarine	1 tbsp.	15 mL
Pepper, sprinkle		
Chopped chives	1 tbsp.	15 mL
Dill weed	¼ tsp.	1 mL

Combine cucumber, boiling water and salt in saucepan. Cover. Cook about 10 minutes until tender. Drain.

Add butter, pepper, chives and dill weed. Toss. Serves 4 to 6.

Pictured on page 53.

HUSH PUPPIES

Solid textured and dark golden brown, these are traditionally served with seafood in southern United States. Like a deep-fried muffin.

Large egg	1	1
Granulated sugar	2 tsp.	10 mL
Baking powder	1 tbsp.	15 mL
Salt	3/4 tsp.	4 mL
Onion powder	1/4 tsp.	1 mL
White cornmeal (or yellow)	1 cup	250 mL
All-purpose flour	1 cup	250 mL
Milk or water	3/4 cup	175 mL

Fat for deep-frying

Beat egg in bowl until frothy.

Add next 7 ingredients. Stir.

Drop by large teaspoonfuls into hot 375°F (190°C) fat. Brown well. This will take about 5 minutes. Check one by breaking open to see if it is cooked in the center. Instead of ball shapes, dough can be pressed into cylinder shapes. Drain on paper towels. Serve hot with any seafood. Makes about 2 dozen.

Pictured on cover.

PARSLEY BUTTER

Put a dab on each plate beside fish serving or spread it over fish.

Butter or hard margarine	1/4 cup	60 mL
Chopped fresh parsley	2 tbsp.	30 mL
Chopped chives	1 tsp.	5 mL
Onion salt	1/8 tsp.	0.5 mL

Mix all ingredients well in small bowl. Chill for 2 to 3 hours so flavors can mingle. Makes 1/4 cup (60 mL).

WHITE BUTTER

Exceptionally good served on broiled fish.

Chopped chives	2 tsp.	10 mL
White vinegar	½ cup	125 mL
Butter or hard margarine	½ cup	125 mL
Salt	½ tsp.	2 mL
Pepper	⅛ tsp.	0.5 mL

Put chives and vinegar into small saucepan. Bring to a boil. Simmer until almost all vinegar has evaporated. Remove from heat. Cool. Set pan in cold water to hasten cooling.

Mix in butter, bit by bit, then add salt and pepper. Mix well. Top hot broiled fish with generous dab. Makes ½ cup (125 mL).

FLATBREAD CRACKERS

Crunchy with sesame seeds. A mild, tasty cracker. Use with soups and chowders as well as for spreads and dips.

Whole wheat flour	1 cup	250 mL
All-purpose flour	1 cup	250 mL
Oat bran	½ cup	125 mL
Sesame seeds	½ cup	125 mL
Cooking oil	⅓ cup	75 mL
Brown sugar	1 tbsp.	15 mL
Salt	½ tsp.	2 mL
Baking soda	½ tsp.	2 mL
White vinegar	2¼ tsp.	11 mL
Milk, add to make	¾ cup	175 mL

Measure first 8 ingredients into bowl. Mix well.

Put vinegar into measuring cup. Add milk to measure ¾ cup (175 mL). Let stand 5 minutes. Pour over ingredients in bowl. Mix well. Roll out quite thin on lightly floured surface. Cut into 2 inch (5 cm) squares. Arrange on ungreased baking sheet. Bake in 350°F (175°C) oven for about 20 minutes until golden. Makes 5 dozen.

Pictured on page 17.

The most popular stuffing for any fish.

Hard margarine (butter browns too fast)	3 tbsp.	50 mL
Chopped onion	½ cup	125 mL
Chopped celery	¼ cup	60 mL
Dry bread crumbs	1 cup	250 mL
Salt	½ tsp.	2 mL
Pepper	⅛ tsp.	0.5 mL
Parsley flakes	½ tsp.	2 mL
Poultry seasoning	½ tsp.	2 mL
Water	3 tbsp.	50 mL

Melt margarine in frying pan. Add onion and celery. Sauté until soft. Remove from heat.

Add remaining ingredients. Stir well. Makes enough to stuff a 4 pound (1.8 kg) fish.

YOUR OWN SMOKED FISH

Dark color and looks like the real thing. Has a good smoked flavor. Try your catch a different way.

Large fish fillets	2¼ lbs.	1 kg
Soy sauce	⅔ cup	150 mL
Llquld smoke	3 tbsp.	50 mL

Place a rack in baking sheet with sides. Lay fillets on rack.

Stir soy sauce and liquid smoke together in small bowl. Brush fillets on both sides. Bake, uncovered, in 325°F (160°C) oven for 1 hour, basting both sides every 15 minutes. Turn carefully as fillets will break apart easily. When 1 hour is up, drain any juice. Return to oven for 5 minutes more to dry a bit. Allow ⅓ pound (150 g) per serving. Serves 6.

RAINBOW BLUEFISH

A rainbow of colors over fillets. This is so low in calories you will feel saintly while eating.

Hard margarine (butter browns too fast)	2 tbsp.	30 mL
Green pepper, seeded and cut in thin strips	1	1
Red pepper, seeded and cut in thin strips	1	1
Yellow pepper, seeded and cut in thin strips	1	1
Medium onion, thinly sliced and quartered	1	1
Zucchini, with peel, about 7 inches (18 cm) long, slivered	1	1
Large tomato, seeded and cubed	1	1
Apple juice	$2/3$ cup	150 mL
Salt	$1/2$ tsp.	2 mL
Pepper	$1/4$ tsp.	1 mL
Cornstarch	2 tsp.	10 mL
Water	2 tsp.	10 mL
Boston bluefish fillets	2 lbs.	900 g
Water, to cover		
Chicken bouillon powder	1 tbsp.	15 mL

Melt margarine in frying pan. Add green, red and yellow peppers and onion. Stir. Cover. Simmer for 5 minutes. You may need to do this in 2 batches. Add more margarine as needed. Remove cover. Stir-fry a bit longer if vegetables are too firm. Remove to bowl.

Add zucchini and tomato to frying pan along with more margarine if needed. Stir-fry until soft. Return pepper mixture to frying pan.

Stir in apple juice, salt and pepper. Bring to a simmer.

Mix cornstarch into water. Stir into simmering vegetables until it returns to a simmer. Cover and keep warm.

Place fish fillets in large saucepan. Add water to cover. Stir in bouillon powder. Cover. Bring to a boil. Simmer gently about 5 minutes until fish flakes when tested with fork. Transfer fish fillets to warm platter. Spoon pepper mixture over fillets. Serves 6.

Pictured on page 71.

This makes an elegant meal. Bake in one pan or in individual casseroles.

CRÊPES

Large eggs	2	2
Milk	2 cups	500 mL
All-purpose flour	2 cups	500 mL
Salt	1/4 tsp.	1 mL
Granulated sugar	1/4 tsp.	1 mL
Cooking oil	1/4 cup	60 mL

SEAFOOD FILLING

Scallops, quartered if large	1 lb.	454 g
Water	1 cup	250 mL
Medium shrimp, peeled and deveined	1 lb.	454 g
Water	1 cup	250 mL
Hard margarine (butter browns too fast)	3 tbsp.	50 mL
Sliced fresh mushrooms	4 cups	1 L
All-purpose flour	3 tbsp.	50 mL
Salt	1/2 tsp.	2 mL
Pepper	1/8 tsp.	0.5 mL
Onion powder	1/4 tsp.	1 mL
Milk (or light cream)	1 1/2 cups	375 mL
Reserved scallop juice		

Crêpes: Put all 6 ingredients into blender. Process until smooth. Fry in hot greased crêpe pan using about 2 tbsp. (30 mL) per crêpe. Makes 12.

Seafood Filling: Simmer scallops in first amount of water in tightly covered saucepan for 3 to 5 minutes until white and opaque. Drain and reserve juice.

Simmer shrimp in second amount of water in tightly covered saucepan for 2 to 4 minutes until pinkish and curled. Drain.

Melt margarine in frying pan. Add mushrooms. Sauté until soft. This is easier to do in 2 batches.

Mix in flour, salt, pepper and onion powder. Stir in milk and scallop juice until it boils and thickens. Measure 1/2 cup (125 mL) and reserve for topping. Add scallops and shrimp to mixture in frying pan. Stir. Measure filling. Divide evenly among 12 crêpes placing off center. Roll crêpe snugly around filling. Place seam side down in greased shallow baking dish just large enough to hold 1 layer. Pour reserved sauce over center of crêpes. Bake, uncovered, in 350°F (175°C) oven for 20 to 25 minutes until hot. Serves 6 people, 2 crêpes each.

SEAFOOD LASAGNE

The addition of fish fillets stretches the seafood. Freezes well. Very good.

Lasagne noodles	8	8
Boiling water	4 qts.	4 L
Cooking oil	1 tbsp.	15 mL
Salt	1 tbsp.	15 mL
Hard margarine (butter browns too fast)	2 tbsp.	30 mL
Chopped onion	1¼ cups	300 mL
Chopped green pepper	¼ cup	60 mL
Chopped celery	¼ cup	60 mL
Cream cheese, cut up	8 oz.	250 mL
Creamed cottage cheese	1 cup	250 mL
Large egg	1	1
Grated Parmesan cheese	¼ cup	60 mL
Salt	½ tsp.	2 mL
Pepper	⅛ tsp.	0.5 mL
Condensed cream of chicken soup	10 oz.	284 mL
Milk	⅓ cup	75 mL
Small cooked shrimp (or 2 x 4 oz., 2 x 113 g cans, rinsed and drained)	2 cups	500 mL
Boston bluefish or cod fillets, cubed	1 lb.	454 g
Whole oregano	1 tsp.	5 mL
Grated Parmesan cheese	¼ cup	60 mL
Grated mozzarella cheese	2 cups	500 mL

Cook lasagne noodles in boiling water, cooking oil and salt in large uncovered pot for 14 to 16 minutes until tender but firm. Drain.

Melt margarine in frying pan. Add onion, green pepper and celery. Sauté until soft.

Stir in cream cheese to melt.

Mix next 5 ingredients in bowl. Add onion mixture. Stir.

(continued on next page)

Stir soup and milk vigorously in separate bowl. Add shrimp, fish and oregano. Stir. To assemble, layer in greased 9 x 13 inch (22 x 33 cm) pan as follows:
1. Layer of noodles
2. All cottage cheese mixture
3. Layer of noodles
4. All fish mixture
5. Parmesan cheese
6. Mozzarella cheese

Cover with greased foil. Bake in 350°F (175°C) oven for 60 minutes. Remove foil. Continue to bake for 5 to 10 minutes to brown lightly. Cuts into 12 pieces. Serves 8.

STUFFED SALMON

Not your usual stuffing. Light colored, nutty and fruity. Freeze stuffing separately.

RAISIN STUFFING

Grated carrot	½ cup	125 mL
Long grain rice	1 cup	250 mL
Chopped onion	1¼ cups	300 mL
Boiling water	2 cups	500 mL
Ground cumin	½ tsp.	2 mL
Salt	1 tsp.	5 mL
Raisins	½ cup	125 mL
Sliced filberts/hazelnuts	3 tbsp.	50 mL
Whole salmon	4 lbs.	1.8 kg

Raisin Stuffing: Measure first 6 ingredients into medium saucepan. Cover. Cook over medium heat for about 15 minutes until rice is tender and water is absorbed.

Stir in raisins and filberts. Remove from heat.

Lay salmon on large piece of greased foil. Stuff with rice mixture. Measure thickest part. Fold foil over salmon sealing completely. Place on ungreased baking sheet for easy handling. Bake in 450°F (230°C) oven for 10 minutes per inch (2.5 cm) of thickness allowing an extra 10 minutes for foil. It should flake when tested with fork. Serves 4 to 6.

SHRIMP CREOLE

A southern dish with a bit of a bite. You can add more cayenne to the sauce to make it as hot as you like.

Hard margarine (butter browns too fast)	2 tbsp.	30 mL
Chopped onion	1 cup	250 mL
Thinly sliced celery	½ cup	125 mL
Chopped green pepper	¼ cup	60 mL
All-purpose flour	2 tbsp.	30 mL
Parsley flakes	½ tsp.	2 mL
Salt	¼ tsp	1 mL
Pepper	⅛ tsp.	0.5 mL
Garlic powder	¼ tsp.	1 mL
Cayenne pepper	¼ tsp.	1 mL
Chicken bouillon powder	2 tsp.	10 mL
Granulated sugar	2 tsp.	10 mL
Water	1 cup	250 mL
Canned tomatoes, broken up	14 oz.	398 mL
Tomato paste	5½ oz.	156 mL
Small bay leaf	1	1
Small or medium cooked shrimp	1 lb.	454 g
RICE		
Long grain rice	1 cup	250 mL
Boiling water	2 cups	500 mL
Salt	½ tsp.	2 mL

Melt margarine in large saucepan. Add onion, celery and green pepper. Sauté until lightly browned.

Mix in next 8 ingredients.

Stir in water until it boils and thickens.

Stir in tomatoes, tomato paste and bay leaf. Cover. Bring to a boil. Simmer gently for 20 minutes, stirring occasionally. Discard bay leaf.

Add shrimp. Cook until hot. Makes 3¼ cups (800 mL) sauce.

Rice: Add rice to boiling salted water in saucepan. Cover. Simmer for about 15 minutes until rice is tender and water is absorbed. Turn out onto warmed platter. Shape into a ring. Pour shrimp mixture into center. Serves 4.

FINFISH CREOLE: Omit shrimp. Cut 1 lb. (454 g) fish fillets of your choice into 1 inch (2.5 cm) squares. Add and simmer about 5 minutes more until fish flakes when tested with fork.

A showy piece with a tasty sauce.

Large eggs	2	2
Canned salmon, drained	2 × 7½ oz.	2 × 213 g
Milk	¾ cup	175 mL
Finely chopped celery	½ cup	125 mL
Minced onion	2 tbsp.	30 mL
Dry bread crumbs	2 cups	500 mL
Lemon juice, fresh or bottled	1 tbsp.	15 mL
Salt	½ tsp.	2 mL
Pepper	¼ tsp.	1 mL
DILL SAUCE		
Hard margarine (butter browns too fast)	3 tbsp.	50 mL
Finely chopped onion	3 tbsp.	50 mL
All-purpose flour	3 tbsp.	50 mL
Salt	½ tsp.	2 mL
Pepper	⅛ tsp.	0.5 mL
Milk	1½ cups	375 mL
Dill weed or tarragon	¼ tsp.	1 mL

Beat eggs in bowl until frothy. Remove skin and round bones from salmon. Mix salmon and next 7 ingredients into eggs. Pack in greased 4 cup (1 L) ring. Bake in 350°F (175°C) oven for 35 to 40 minutes until set.

Dill Sauce: Melt margarine in saucepan. Add onion. Sauté until clear.

Mix in flour, salt and pepper. Stir in milk until it boils and thickens.

Add dill weed. Add more milk to thin sauce if desired. Turn out Salmon Ring onto plate. Spoon sauce over top or serve on the side. Serves 4 to 6.

Pictured on page 71.

BLUEFISH FANCY

There is something fishy about this Cordon Bleu. It is made with fish instead of chicken and cooked flat rather than rolled. Fabulous.

All-purpose flour	3 tbsp.	50 mL
Salt	1/2 tsp.	2 mL
Pepper	1/8 tsp.	0.5 mL
Paprika	1/2 tsp.	2 mL
Butter or hard margarine	2 tbsp.	30 mL
Boston bluefish fillets	1 1/4 lbs.	568 g
Cooked ham slices, cut to fit	3	3
Mozzarella cheese slices, cut to fit	3	3
Paprika, sprinkle		

Mix first 4 ingredients in small bowl.

Melt butter in frying pan.

Dip fillets in flour mixture. Arrange in frying pan. Brown underside. Turn. Brown other side.

Cover each fillet with ham, then cheese. Sprinkle with paprika. Cover. Cook for about 2 minutes until fish flakes and cheese is melted. Serves 4.

1. Paella page 86
2. Cucumber Veggie page 42
3. Salmon Dorie page 96
4. Fish In Brown Butter page 63
5. Shrimp Sauced Sole page 59

Casserole Dish Courtesy Of:
Artifacts

Dinnerware Courtesy Of:
Le Gnome

Stained Glass Courtesy Of:
Winter Art Glass

Spinach base gives a colorful touch to this. With a golden brown topping, it looks and tastes great. It can be stretched to serve one or two more by dividing spinach into more piles.

MORNAY SAUCE

Butter or hard margarine	¹⁄₄ cup	60 mL
All-purpose flour	¹⁄₄ cup	60 mL
Chicken bouillon powder	1 tsp.	5 mL
Evaporated skim milk (or light cream)	13¹⁄₂ oz.	385 mL
Grated Parmesan cheese	¹⁄₃ cup	75 mL
Frozen spinach, cooked, drained and coarsely chopped	10 oz.	284 g
Butter or hard margarine	2 tbsp.	30 mL
Lemon juice, fresh or bottled	4 tsp.	20 mL
Flounder fillets	1¹⁄₂ lbs.	680 g

Salt, sprinkle
Pepper, sprinkle

Lemon wedges and parsley, for garnish

Mornay Sauce: Melt first amount of butter in saucepan. Mix in flour and bouillon powder. Stir in evaporated milk until it boils and thickens.

Add Parmesan cheese. Stir. Cover and remove from heat.

Mix 1 cup (250 mL) Mornay Sauce with spinach. Cover to keep warm.

Melt second amount of butter and lemon juice in small saucepan.

Arrange fillets skin side down on greased broiler tray. Brush with butter-lemon mixture. Broil on top rack for 4 minutes. Brush with butter-lemon mixture again. Broil about 4 minutes more, until fish flakes when tested with fork.

Sprinkle fillets with salt and pepper. On greased broiler-proof platter or tray, spoon spinach in 4 piles. Put fish fillet on top of each. Divide remaining Mornay Sauce over top. Broil about 2 to 3 minutes until sauce is golden.

Garnish with lemon wedges and parsley. Serves 4.

Pictured on page 89.

SHRIMP MARINARA

Spaghetti covered with shrimp in a dark red sauce. Sauce can be kept frozen, ready to use on freshly cooked pasta.

SAUCE

Cooking oil	1 tbsp.	15 mL
Chopped onion	½ cup	125 mL
Canned tomatoes, broken up	28 oz.	796 mL
Tomato paste	5½ oz.	156 mL
Granulated sugar	1 tsp.	5 mL
Sweet basil	1 tsp.	5 mL
Whole oregano	½ tsp.	2 mL
Parsley flakes	1 tsp.	5 mL
Salt	½ tsp.	2 mL
Pepper	¼ tsp.	1 mL
Garlic powder	¼ tsp.	1 mL
Medium shrimp, peeled and deveined	1 lb.	454 g

PASTA

Spaghetti	8 oz.	250 g
Boiling water	3 qts.	3 L
Cooking oil	1 tbsp.	15 mL
Salt	2 tsp.	10 mL

Grated Parmesan cheese, sprinkle

Sauce: Heat cooking oil in large saucepan. Add onion. Sauté until soft.

Add next 9 ingredients. Stir. Bring to a boil. Simmer slowly, uncovered, for 30 minutes, stirring frequently, until quite thick.

Add shrimp. Return to a boil. Cover. Cook 4 to 5 minutes until shrimp have curled a bit and are pinkish in color. Set aside. Keep warm.

Pasta: Cook spaghetti in boiling water, cooking oil and salt in large uncovered pot for 11 to13 minutes until tender but firm. Drain. Divide among 4 plates. Spoon sauce over top. Serves 4.

The tomato sauce over white pasta rolls makes quite a contrast. Allow a bit of extra time to fill and roll.

Lasagne noodles	6	6
Boiling water	3 qts.	3 L
Cooking oil	1 tbsp.	15 mL
Salt	2 tsp.	10 mL
FILLING		
Dry curd cottage cheese	1 cup	250 mL
Large egg	1	1
Grated Parmesan cheese	1/4 cup	60 mL
Chopped chives	1 tbsp.	15 mL
Onion powder	1/4 tsp.	1 mL
Crabmeat (or 1 can 4.2 oz., 120 g, drained), membrane removed	1 cup	250 mL
TOMATO SAUCE		
Canned tomatoes, broken up	14 oz.	398 mL
Tomato sauce	7 1/2 oz.	213 mL
Chopped onion	1/2 cup	125 mL
Bay leaf	1	1
Whole oregano	1/2 tsp.	2 mL
Sweet basil	1/4 tsp.	1 mL
Granulated sugar	1 tsp.	5 mL
Garlic powder	1/4 tsp.	1 mL

Grated Parmesan cheese, sprinkle

Cook noodles in boiling water, cooking oil and salt in large uncovered pot about 14 to 16 minutes until tender but firm. Drain. Rinse in cold water. Drain.

Filling: Mash cottage cheese and egg with fork.

Add first amount of Parmesan cheese, chives, onion powder and crabmeat. Mash well. Divide among noodles. Spread to cover each noodle. Roll up tightly. Lay seam side down in greased 8 x 8 inch (20 x 20 cm) pan.

Tomato Sauce: Measure first 8 ingredients into saucepan. Heat, stirring often, until it boils. Simmer for 15 to 20 minutes. Discard bay leaf. Pour sauce over rolls in pan.

Sprinkle with Parmesan cheese. Cover. Bake in 375°F (190°C) oven for about 30 minutes. Makes 6 servings.

Pictured on page 89.

BASIL LINGCOD FILLETS

Decorated with red tomato slices, these are spiced for contentment.
A good light recipe.

Lingcod fillets	1½ lbs.	680 g
Lemon juice, fresh or bottled	4 tsp.	20 mL
Salt, sprinkle		
Pepper, sprinkle		
Tomato slices (not too thick)	24	24
Butter or hard margarine	2 tbsp.	30 mL
Finely chopped onion	½ cup	125 mL
Chopped green onion	2 tbsp.	30 mL
Sweet basil	¼ tsp.	1 mL
Salt	⅛ tsp.	0.5 mL
Grated Parmesan cheese, sprinkle		
Lemon wedges, for garnish	4	4

Arrange fish fillets in single layer in greased 9 x 13 inch (22 x 33 cm) pan. Sprinkle with lemon juice, salt and pepper. Layer tomato slices over fillets.

Melt butter in frying pan. Add onion. Sauté until soft.

Add green onion, basil and salt. Sprinkle evenly over tomato slices.

Sprinkle lightly with cheese. Cover pan with foil. Bake in 400°F (205°C) oven for about 20 minutes until fish flakes easily when fork tested.

Garnish with lemon wedges to serve. Serves 4.

Paré Pointer

See all those baby bushes in the garden? It's a tree nursery.

The sauce raises this to a special meal. Appetizing.

Butter or hard margarine	1 tbsp.	15 mL
All-purpose flour	1½ tsp.	7 mL
Salt	½ tsp.	2 mL
Onion powder	⅛ tsp.	0.5 mL
Cayenne pepper	⅛ tsp.	0.5 mL
Prepared horseradish	¼ tsp.	1 mL
Milk	½ cup	125 mL
Small or medium cooked shrimp (or 1 can 4 oz., 113 g, rinsed and drained)	1 cup	250 mL
Sole fillets	1½ lbs.	680 g
TOPPING		
Butter or hard margarine	2 tbsp.	30 mL
Lemon juice, fresh or bottled	1 tsp.	5 mL
Parsley flakes	¼ tsp.	1 mL

Paprika, sprinkle

Lemon wedges, for garnish

Melt butter in small saucepan. Mix in next 5 ingredients. Stir in milk until it boils and thickens. Remove from heat.

Add shrimp. Stir.

Place sole fillets in greased baking dish large enough to hold single layer. Spoon shrimp mixture over fillets.

Topping: Melt butter in small saucepan. Stir in lemon juice and parsley. Drizzle over shrimp mixture.

Sprinkle with paprika. Bake, uncovered, in 350°F (175°C) oven for about 25 minutes until fish flakes easily when tested with fork.

Add lemon wedges to serve. Makes 4 servings.

Pictured on page 53.

CRAB SAUCED SOLE: Use crabmeat in place of shrimp.

SEA BASS BAKE

Covered with brandy flavored dressing, sprinkled with Parmesan and baked. Good flavor.

Sea bass fillets	1½ lbs.	680 g
Salad dressing (or mayonnaise)	⅓ cup	75 mL
Brandy flavoring	1 tsp.	5 mL
Pepper	1/16 tsp.	0.5 mL

Grated Parmesan cheese, sprinkle

Arrange fillets in greased pan large enough to hold single layer.

Combine salad dressing, brandy flavoring and pepper in small bowl. Stir. Spread over fish fillets.

Sprinkle with Parmesan cheese. Bake, uncovered, in 350°F (175°C) oven for about 25 minutes until fish flakes when tested with fork. Serves 4.

MOCK LOBSTER

You're in for a surprise and a treat. This can also be used with a more delicate textured fish such as cod.

Monkfish fillets (or shark)	1 lb.	454 g
Salt	2 tbsp.	30 mL
Cold water, to cover		
White vinegar	2 tbsp.	30 mL
Peppercorns	4	4
Small bay leaf	½	½
Cold water, to cover		
Butter or hard margarine, melted (butter is best for flavor)	¼ cup	60 mL

Place fillets and salt in saucepan. Cover with water. Bring to a boil. Simmer gently for 10 minutes. Drain.

Add vinegar, peppercorns and ½ bay leaf. Cover with water once more. Bring to a boil. Simmer gently for 10 minutes. Drain. Cut into bite size pieces.

Dip each piece in melted butter. Makes 4 servings.

A small quantity. Just right for a snack.

Medium potatoes, peeled and quartered	2	2
Boiling salted water, to cover		
Hard margarine (butter browns too fast)	1 tbsp.	15 mL
Chopped green pepper	¼ cup	60 mL
Finely chopped onion	½ cup	125 mL
Worcestershire sauce	¼ tsp.	1 mL
Salt	½ tsp.	2 mL
Pepper	¼ tsp.	1 mL
Paprika	¼ tsp.	1 mL
Canned salmon, (red, such as sockeye, is best for color), drained	7½ oz.	213 g

Cook potatoes in salted water until tender when pierced with tip of sharp knife. Drain. Cool. Dice ¼ inch (6 mm) size.

Melt margarine in frying pan. Add green pepper and onion. Sauté until soft.

Stir in Worcestershire sauce, salt, pepper and paprika. Add diced potato.

Remove skin and round bones from salmon. Flake and add salmon. Stir to mix. Allow to brown a bit. Makes 3 cups (750 mL).

Paré Pointer

His jacket went up in flames. It was a blazer.

OVEN CRISP FISH

So tasty with Parmesan cheese. So crunchy with crushed corn flakes. A special treat.

Cooking oil	¼ cup	60 mL
Salt	¼ tsp.	1 mL
Pepper	⅛ tsp.	0.5 mL
Seasoned salt	¼ tsp.	1 mL
Fish fillets, your choice	1½ lbs.	680 g
Grated Parmesan cheese, sprinkle		
Crushed corn flakes	½ cup	125 mL

Combine cooking oil, salt, pepper and seasoned salt in small bowl.

Brush both sides of fillets with oil mixture. Place fillets in shallow bowl. Pour remaining cooking oil mixture over top. Marinate for 15 minutes.

Remove fillets from marinade. Sprinkle lightly with Parmesan cheese. Dip in crushed corn flakes. Arrange in single layer in greased baking pan. If you line pan with greased foil, it helps with clean up. Bake in 450°F (230°C) oven for 12 to 15 minutes until fish flakes when tested with a fork. Serves 4.

BAKED SWORDFISH

What a treat this is! The brown topping of dry onion soup mix does the trick. So simple and delicious. No bones to contend with.

Swordfish or shark fillets	4	4
Butter or hard margarine	¼ cup	60 mL
Envelope dry onion soup mix	1 × 1½ oz.	1 × 42 g
Barbecue sauce	2 tbsp.	30 mL

Arrange fillets in small roaster.

Melt butter in small saucepan. Stir in onion soup mix and barbecue sauce. Pour over fillets. Cover roaster tightly. Bake in 350°F (175°C) oven for 20 to 25 minutes until tender. Serves 4.

Pictured on page 89.

BAKED HALIBUT: Cut a thick halibut fillet into serving portions. Use instead of swordfish. Excellent.

Buttery delicious.

All-purpose flour	¼ cup	60 mL
Salt	½ tsp.	2 mL
Pepper	⅛ tsp.	0.5 mL
Paprika	¼ tsp.	1 mL
Onion powder	⅛ tsp.	0.5 mL
Hard margarine (butter browns too fast)	2 tbsp.	30 mL
Fish fillets or steaks of your choice	4	4

BROWN BUTTER SAUCE

Butter or hard margarine	¼ cup	60 mL
Lemon juice, fresh or bottled	1 tbsp.	15 mL
Fresh parsley, for garnish		
Lemon wedges, for garnish	4	4

Stir first 5 ingredients in shallow bowl.

Melt margarine in frying pan. Coat both sides of fish fillets with flour mixture. Add to frying pan. Brown both sides on medium-high until fish flakes when tested with fork. Transfer to heated plates or serving dish.

Brown Butter Sauce: Heat butter in frying pan until it turns a light brown. Remove from heat.

Stir in lemon juice. Pour over fish.

Garnish with parsley and lemon. Serves 4.

Pictured on page 53.

A pencil would easily win a race with paper. Paper remains stationery.

CARAMELIZED FILLETS

Such a pleasing dish. The flavor of caramelized onion gives the fish a wonderful taste.

Brown sugar, packed	3 tbsp.	50 mL
White vinegar	2 tbsp.	30 mL
Cooking oil	1 tbsp.	15 mL
Turmeric	1/8 tsp.	0.5 mL
Prepared mustard	1/4 tsp.	1 mL
Salt	1/4 tsp.	1 mL
Large onions, sliced in rings (about 1 lb., 454 g)	2	2
Catfish fillets, or other fish	1 1/4 lbs.	560 g

Measure first 6 ingredients into frying pan. Stir.

Add onion. Cook slowly on medium-low until tender and caramelized. Liquid will be almost gone. Onions should be deep golden in color. This will take about 10 minutes.

Spoon about 1/2 of onion mixture in pan large enough to hold fish in single layer. Arrange fish over top. Spoon remaining onion over top. Cover tightly. Bake in 400°F (205°C) oven for 20 to 25 minutes until fish flakes. Serves 4.

BACON FISH STICKS

The only way to improve on this is to wrap two pieces of bacon around the fish stick.

Bacon slices	4	4
Frozen breaded fish sticks	8	8

Fry bacon until about half cooked. Cut slices in half crosswise.

Wrap each fish stick with half slice of bacon. Place seam side down on ungreased baking sheet. Bake in 450°F (230°C) oven for 14 to 16 minutes, turning to cook and brown both sides. May also be cooked on barbecue. Makes 8 bacon-wrapped fish sticks.

A novel way to use smoked fish. These browned cakes are excellent.

Potatoes, peeled and quartered (3 medium)	1½ lbs.	680 g
Chopped onion	½ cup	125 mL
Boiling water		
Smoked fillets of your choice	1 lb.	454 g
Water, to cover		
Large egg	1	1
Fine dry bread crumbs	¼ cup	60 mL
Butter or hard margarine, melted	1 tbsp.	15 mL
Salt	½ tsp.	2 mL
Pepper	⅛ tsp.	0.5 mL
Hard margarine (butter browns too fast)	2 tbsp.	30 mL

Cook potato and onion in boiling water until tender. Drain. Mash together.

Cover smoked fillets with water. Bring to a boil. Simmer slowly for about 10 minutes until fish flakes. Drain. Cool until you can handle. Flake fish. Add to potato mixture. Stir.

Beat egg in small bowl. Stir in bread crumbs, butter, salt and pepper. Add to potato mixture. Stir. Shape into patties. An ice cream scoop works great for measuring.

Melt margarine in frying pan. Fry patties, browning each side and heating through completely. Makes about 13 fish cakes.

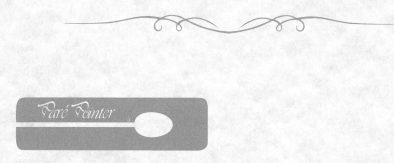

Paré Pointer

Batman searched the woods to see if he could find a Robin.

OCEAN PERCH

This simple mixture gives a gentle boost to the flavor of the fillets.
Very easy.

Lemon juice, fresh or bottled	2 tbsp.	30 mL
Dill weed	1/4 tsp	1 mL
Onion powder	1/4 tsp.	1 mL
Salt	1/4 tsp.	1 mL
Pepper	1/4 tsp.	1 mL
Paprika	1/4 tsp.	1 mL
Ocean perch fillets	1 1/2 lbs.	680 g
Hard margarine (butter browns too fast)	2 tbsp.	30 mL

Stir first 6 ingredients in small cup.

Brush over both sides of fillets.

Melt margarine in frying pan. Arrange fillets in frying pan skin side down. Turn when browned. Brown other side. Total time should be about 5 minutes depending on thickness. Check thickest part of fillet to see if it flakes when tested with fork. Serves 4.

OVEN BAKED PICKEREL

A slightly tangy sauce dresses this fish. Only three ingredients.

Pickerel (also called walleye) fillets	6	6
Condensed cream of mushroom soup	10 oz.	284 mL
Dijon mustard	4 tsp.	20 mL

Arrange fillets in ungreased baking pan large enough to hold single layer. Cover. Bake in 400°F (205°C) oven for 10 minutes.

Stir soup and mustard together in bowl. Spoon over fillets being sure to get some on every one. Cover. Bake 10 minutes more. Serves 6.

Potatoes are cooked in the oven with very little fat. A pleasantly different fish and chips dish.

Cooking oil	2 tbsp.	30 mL
Garlic powder, just a pinch		
Medium potatoes, peeled and sliced into long strips (French fry style)	4	4
Salt, sprinkle		
Pepper, sprinkle		
Cod fillets	1½ lbs.	680 g
Cooking oil	1½ tbsp.	25 mL
Garlic powder, just a pinch		
Salt, sprinkle		
Pepper, sprinkle		

Mix first amount of cooking oil and garlic powder in large bowl.

Add potato. Toss together well to coat. Arrange on ungreased baking sheet with sides.

Sprinkle with salt and pepper. Bake, uncovered, in 450°F (230°C) oven for 15 minutes. Turn strips over.

Lay fish fillets over potato.

Stir second amounts of cooking oil and garlic powder in small cup. Brush over fish fillets.

Sprinkle fish with salt and pepper. Bake for 10 to 15 minutes more until fish flakes when tested with fork. Serves 4.

Combine an automobile and a candle and then you'll have car wax.

COD VERONIQUE

White fish covered with a greenish grape sauce. Not your usual fare.
Wonderful company food.

Cod fillets	1½ lbs.	680 g
Water, to cover		
SAUCE		
Water	¾ cup	175 mL
White wine (or alcohol-free wine)	¼ cup	60 mL
Green onions, chopped	2	2
Chicken bouillon powder	1 tbsp.	15 mL
Cornstarch	2 tbsp.	30 mL
Water	¼ cup	60 mL
Halved seedless green grapes	1 cup	250 mL
Lemon juice, fresh or bottled	1 tsp.	5 mL
Salt	¼ tsp.	1 mL
Pepper	⅛ tsp.	0.5 mL

Place fillets and first amount of water in large saucepan. Cover. Bring to a boil. Simmer gently for 7 to 10 minutes until fish flakes when tested with fork. Drain. Keep warm.

Sauce: Combine first 4 ingredients in small saucepan. Boil gently for about 2 minutes to cook onion slightly.

Mix cornstarch and third amount of water in small cup. Stir into boiling mixture until it returns to a boil and thickens.

Stir in grapes, lemon juice, salt and pepper. Stir and heat through. Spoon sauce over fish. Serves 4.

Paré Pointer

People who become printers turn out to be the right type.

A colorful tomato based sauce. Very tasty.

Medium tomatoes, cut in chunks	3	3
Tomato juice	⅓ cup	75 mL
Canned sliced mushrooms, drained	10 oz.	284 mL
Granulated sugar	½ tsp.	2 mL
Sweet basil	½ tsp.	2 mL
Garlic powder	¼ tsp.	1 mL
Ground thyme, just a pinch		
Salt	½ tsp.	2 mL
Pepper	¼ tsp.	1 mL
Canned artichoke hearts, drained and quartered	14 oz.	398 mL
Cod or snapper fillets, cut in chunks	1 lb.	454 g

Hot pepper sauce, few drops

Combine first 9 ingredients in large pot or Dutch oven. Bring to a boil, stirring occasionally. Sauce will stay thin.

Add artichoke hearts and fish chunks. Cover. Return to a simmer. Simmer for 5 minutes or until fish flakes.

Add hot pepper sauce, 2 drops at a time, until it's the right taste for you. Serves 4.

Paré Pointer

No one knows how rabbits make beer except they have lots of hops to start.

BLACKENED SNAPPER

Cook this on the barbecue so the household smoke detector doesn't sound. Spicy hot and spicy delicious.

CAJUN COATING

Salt	1 tbsp.	15 mL
Paprika	1 tbsp.	15 mL
Onion powder	1 tbsp.	15 mL
Garlic powder	1 tbsp.	15 mL
Ground thyme	2 tsp.	10 mL
Whole oregano	1 tsp.	10 mL
Pepper	½ tsp.	2 mL
Cayenne pepper	¾ tsp.	4 mL
Chili powder	½ tsp.	2 mL
Celery salt	½ tsp.	2 mL
Snapper fillets (or other thin fillets)	2½ lbs.	1 kg
Cooking oil	2 tbsp.	30 mL

Cajun Coating: Measure first 10 ingredients into small bowl. Stir.

Heat heavy frying pan, cast iron if possible, until very hot. Drops of water should dance on it when tested. Do not use a coated pan. Blot fillets with paper towel. Brush both sides with cooking oil. Dip into seasoning to coat both sides. Put into hot pan. Cook 2 to 3 minutes per side. Serves 6.

1. Rainbow Bluefish page 46
2. Lemon Garlic Shrimp page 74
3. Salmon Ring page 51
4. Sesame Sole page 78
5. Fruited Shark page 96
6. Dilled Sauce page 138

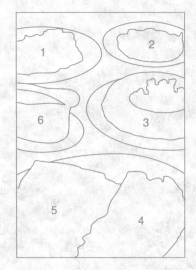

China Courtesy Of:
Enchanted Kitchen

SAUCED SALMON

A delicate sauce adds richness to these steaks. An easy addition.

Salmon steaks	4	4
Boiling water, to cover		
White wine (or alcohol-free wine)	¼ cup	60 mL
Chopped green onion	3 tbsp.	50 mL
Whipping cream	1 cup	250 mL

Place salmon in large pot. Add boiling water to cover. Barely simmer with lid on pot for about 10 minutes until fish flakes when tested with fork.

Meanwhile combine wine, onion and cream in heavy saucepan. Bring to a boil, stirring often. Stir and boil until it reduces and thickens. Spoon over salmon steaks. Serves 4.

SHANTUNG SHRIMP

A quick snack for two. Flavored with ginger and wine.

Ketchup	3 tbsp.	50 mL
White wine (or alcohol-free wine)	1 tbsp.	15 mL
Chili sauce	1 tsp.	5 mL
Granulated sugar	1 tsp.	5 mL
Salt	¼ tsp.	1 mL
Ground ginger	⅛ tsp.	0.5 mL
Canned medium shrimp, juice reserved	4 oz.	113 g
Reserved juice	2 tbsp.	30 mL

Measure first 6 ingredients into saucepan.

Add shrimp and reserved juice to saucepan. Heat, stirring occasionally, until hot. Serves 2.

Paré Pointer

The banker quit his job because he was bored. He lost interest in everything.

POLYNESIAN SHRIMP

Surrounded by pineapple and green pepper with a rich looking sweet and sour sauce. Serve over rice or noodles. Freezes well.

Hard margarine (butter browns too fast)	1 tbsp.	15 mL
Green pepper, seeded and cut in slivers	1	1
Canned pineapple chunks, with juice	14 oz.	398 mL
Prepared orange juice	½ cup	125 mL
Lemon juice, fresh or bottled	1 tsp.	5 mL
Soy sauce	1 tbsp.	15 mL
Granulated sugar	1 tbsp.	15 mL
Salt	⅛ tsp.	0.5 mL
Cornstarch	1 tbsp.	15 mL
Water	2 tbsp.	30 mL
Medium shrimp, peeled and deveined	1 lb.	454 g
Boiling water, to cover		

Melt margarine in saucepan. Add green pepper. Sauté until tender-crisp.

Add pineapple with juice, orange juice, lemon juice, soy sauce, sugar and salt. Bring to a boil.

Stir cornstarch and water together in small cup. Stir into boiling mixture until it returns to a boil and thickens. Keep warm.

Cook shrimp in boiling water for 3 to 5 minutes until pinkish and curled. Drain. Add to pineapple mixture. Stir. Serves 4.

LEMON GARLIC SHRIMP

Indulge in this attractive dish. Add more garlic to suit your taste.

Cooking oil	1 tbsp.	15 mL
Butter or hard margarine	1 tbsp.	15 mL
Garlic cloves, minced	1-2	1-2
Frozen shrimp, tails intact, peeled and deveined (41 to 50 count)	1 lb.	454 g
Salt, sprinkle		
Green onions, chopped	2	2
Parsley flakes	1 tsp.	5 mL
Lemon juice, fresh or bottled	1 tbsp.	15 mL
Lemon pepper	¼ tsp.	1 mL

(continued on next page)

Heat cooking oil and butter in frying pan. Add garlic. Sauté for 1 minute.

Add shrimp. Stir-fry for about 2 minutes.

Sprinkle generously with salt. Continue to stir-fry for 1 or 2 minutes more until shrimp turn pinkish and curl slightly.

Add remaining 4 ingredients. Stir. Serves 4.

Pictured on page 71.

MACARONI SALMON SQUARES

Add a vegetable and a salad and you have a full meal.

Elbow macaroni	2 cups	500 mL
Boiling water	3 qts.	3 L
Cooking oil	1 tbsp.	15 mL
Salt	2 tsp.	10 mL
Canned salmon, with juice	2 × 7½ oz.	2 × 213 g
Finely chopped onion	½ cup	125 mL
Diced green pepper	¼ cup	60 mL
Parsley flakes	1¼ tsp.	6 mL
Large eggs	2	2
Milk	⅓ cup	75 mL
Salt	1 tsp.	5 mL
Pepper	⅛ tsp.	0.5 mL
Paprika, sprinkle		

Cook macaroni in boiling water, cooking oil and first amount of salt in large uncovered pot for 5 to 7 minutes until tender but firm. Drain. Return macaroni to pot.

Remove skin and round bones from salmon. Flake. Add salmon, onion, green pepper and parsley to macaroni. Mix.

Beat eggs in small mixing bowl until frothy. Mix in milk, second amount of salt, and pepper. Add to macaroni mixture. Stir. Pack in greased 9 × 9 inch (22 × 22 cm) pan.

Sprinkle with paprika. Cover. Bake in 350°F (175°C) oven for about 45 minutes. Let stand for 10 minutes. Serve with White Sauce, page 136. Serves 6.

HADDOCK RAREBIT

A golden cheese topping to this RAB-bit surrounded by little red tomatoes.

All-purpose flour	¼ cup	60 mL
Dry mustard powder	1 tsp.	5 mL
Salt	½ tsp.	2 mL
Evaporated skim milk (or light cream)	1 cup	250 mL
Grated medium Cheddar cheese	1 cup	250 mL
Butter or hard margarine	2 tsp.	10 mL
Haddock fish fillets	1½ lbs.	680 g
Paprika, sprinkle		
GARNISH		
Cherry tomatoes	12	12

Stir flour, mustard and salt in saucepan.

Gradually whisk in milk. Mix until smooth. Heat and stir until it boils and thickens.

Stir in cheese and butter. Stir to melt.

Arrange fillets in pan just large enough to hold single layer. Pour cheese sauce over top.

Sprinkle with paprika. Bake, uncovered, in 350°F (175°C) oven for about 30 minutes until fish flakes when tested with fork.

Garnish: After fillets have cooked for about 15 minutes, place tomatoes in another baking pan in single layer in oven. Bake fillets and tomatoes 15 minutes. Carefully transfer fillets to platter. Place tomatoes here and there beside fillets. Serves 4 to 6.

Paré Pointer

Often you find Eskimos a little husky.

Try this with and without the sauce. It's good either way.

White wine (or alcohol-free wine)	½ cup	125 mL
Snapper fillets	1½ lbs.	680 g
All-purpose flour	⅓ cup	75 mL
Salt	1 tsp.	5 mL
Pepper	¼ tsp.	1 mL
Paprika	1 tsp.	5 mL
Hard margarine (butter browns too fast)	1 tbsp.	15 mL
Medium onion, sliced	1	1

SAUCE		
Butter or hard margarine	2 tbsp.	30 mL
All-purpose flour	1½ tbsp.	25 mL
Salt	½ tsp.	2 mL
Pepper	⅛ tsp.	0.5 mL
Garlic powder	⅛ tsp.	0.5 mL
Ground ginger, just a pinch		
Evaporated skim milk (or light cream)	1 cup	250 mL
Soy sauce	½ tsp.	2 mL

Pour wine over fillets in plastic bag. Let marinate for 30 minutes, turning often.

Mix flour, salt, pepper and paprika in small bowl. Set aside.

Melt margarine in frying pan. Add onion. Sauté until soft. Transfer to small bowl. Keep warm.

Sauce: Melt butter in saucepan. Mix in flour, salt, pepper, garlic powder and ginger. Stir in milk and soy sauce until it boils and thickens. Keep warm.

Drain fillets. Coat with flour mixture. Arrange in frying pan, adding more butter if needed. Brown both sides, cooking until fish flakes when tested with fork. To serve, top fillets with onion. Pour sauce over top. Serves 4.

Paré Pointer

He fixes wheels and bicycles. He's a spokesman.

BOSTON BLUEFISH

Cooked on a bed of vegetables. This is wonderfully different both in flavor and color.

Butter or hard margarine	1 tbsp.	15 mL
Large onion, quartered lengthwise, thinly sliced	1	1
Sliced fresh mushrooms	2 cups	500 mL
Medium tomatoes, coarsely chopped	2	2
Salt	1/4 tsp.	1 mL
Apple juice	1/4 cup	60 mL
Boston bluefish fillets	1 1/2 lbs.	680 g
Salt, sprinkle		
Pepper, sprinkle		

Melt butter in frying pan. Add onion, mushroom and tomato. Sprinkle with first amount of salt. Stir-fry until tomato begins to lose its juice. Cover. Simmer for about 4 minutes until vegetables are soft.

Stir in apple juice. Smooth top of vegetables.

Lay fillets over vegetables. Sprinkle fillets with salt and pepper. Cover. Simmer for about 10 minutes until fish flakes easily when fork tested. Serves 4.

SESAME SOLE

With a sesame seed coating these fillets look so appealing.

All-purpose flour	1/3 cup	75 mL
Large egg	1	1
Water	1 tbsp.	15 mL
Salt	3/4 tsp.	4 mL
Pepper	1/4 tsp.	1 mL
Fine dry bread crumbs	1/3 cup	75 mL
Sesame seeds	1/3 cup	75 mL
Butter or hard margarine	2 tbsp.	30 mL
Sole fillets	1 1/2 lbs.	680 mL

(continued on next page)

Measure flour into small bowl.

Beat egg, water, salt and pepper together with fork in separate small bowl.

Measure bread crumbs into third bowl. Add sesame seeds. Stir.

Melt butter in frying pan. Dip fillets in flour. Dip in egg mixture. Coat with crumb-seed mixture. Arrange in frying pan. Brown both sides, cooking until fish flakes when tested with fork. Serves 4.

Pictured on page 71.

SZECHUAN SHRIMP

Spicy hot in a rich-looking dark sauce. Serve over rice or noodles.

Hard margarine (butter browns too fast)	1 tbsp.	15 mL
Chopped celery	½ cup	125 mL
Medium tomato, diced	1	1
Green onions, chopped	3-4	3-4
Chili sauce	⅓ cup	75 mL
Gravy browner	1 tsp.	5 mL
Ground ginger	½ tsp.	2 mL
Garlic powder	¼ tsp.	1 mL
Cayenne pepper	⅛ tsp.	0.5 mL
Medium shrimp, peeled and deveined	1 lb.	454 g

Melt margarine in saucepan. Add celery. Sauté until soft.

Add tomato and onion. Cook about 2 minutes.

Add next 5 ingredients. Heat. Taste, adding more cayenne if desired.

Stir in shrimp. Cook until bubbly hot and shrimp are pinkish and curled. Serves 4.

Pictured on page 89.

Dracula's favorite ship is a blood vessel.

POACHED TROUT

The shrimp filling is excellent. Use with either cooking method.

POACHING LIQUID

Water	4 cups	1 L
Large onion, cut in chunks	1	1
Coarsely chopped celery	¼ cup	60 mL
Apple juice	2 cups	500 mL
Small bay leaf	1	1
Whole peppercorns	4	4
Whole clove	1	1
Ground thyme, just a pinch		
Whole dressed trout, about ¾ lb. (300 g) each, head removed (or leave on, if desired)	6	6

SHRIMP FILLING

Butter or hard margarine	6 tbsp.	100 mL
All-purpose flour	⅓ cup	75 mL
Salt	½ tsp.	2 mL
Pepper	¼ tsp.	1 mL
Paprika	½ tsp.	2 mL
Onion powder	¼ tsp.	1 mL
Parsley flakes	½ tsp.	2 mL
Milk	2½ cups	625 mL
Sherry (or alcohol-free sherry), optional	2 tbsp.	30 mL
Small cooked shrimp (or 2 × 4 oz., 2 × 113 g cans, rinsed and drained)	2 cups	500 mL

Poaching Liquid: Combine first 8 ingredients in large pot. Bring to a boil. Boil gently for 15 minutes.

Add trout. If liquid doesn't cover trout, add enough water to cover. Return to a simmer. Simmer slowly for about 15 minutes until fish flakes when tested with a fork. Remove skin, if desired, before serving.

Shrimp Filling: Melt butter in saucepan. Mix in flour, salt, pepper, paprika, onion powder and parsley flakes. Stir in milk until it boils and thickens. Add sherry, if desired.

Add shrimp. Stir. Heat through. Fill cooked fish cavities allowing any extra to run onto the plate. Makes 3 cups (750 mL). Serves 6.

PAN FRIED TROUT: Heat 1 tbsp. (15 mL) each of butter or hard margarine and cooking oil. Add dressed trout. Fry and brown both sides until fish flakes when tested with a fork. Remove skin if desired, before filling with Shrimp Filling, above.

An extraordinary flavor. A family favorite.

Hard margarine (butter browns too fast)	2 tbsp.	30 mL
All-purpose flour	2 tbsp.	30 mL
Parsley flakes	1/2 tsp.	2 mL
Whole oregano, just a pinch		
Ground thyme, just a pinch		
Sweet basil, just a pinch		
Celery flakes	1/2 tsp.	2 mL
Chicken bouillon powder	1 tsp.	5 mL
Salt	1/2 tsp.	2 mL
Pepper	1/4 tsp.	1 mL
Evaporated skim milk (or 1 1/2 cups, 375 mL, whipping cream)	13 1/2 oz.	385 ml
Commercial barbecued salmon, diced (about 1/2 lb., 225 g)	1 1/3 cups	325 mL
Medium noodles	1 lb.	454 g
Boiling water	4 qts.	1 L
Cooking oil	1 tbsp.	15 mL
Salt	1 tbsp.	15 mL
Milk, if desired		

Melt margarine in saucepan. Mix in next 9 ingredients. Stir in milk until it boils and thickens.

Add salmon. Stir. Cover and keep warm.

Cook noodles in boiling water, cooking oil and salt In large uncovered pot for 5 to 7 minutes until tender but firm. Drain. Return noodles to pot. Add salmon mixture. Toss. If you want it more moist, stir in a small amount of milk. Makes 8 cups (2 L).

BAKED SALMON STEAKS

A flavorful mushroom-topped steak.

Salmon steaks	4	4
Canned sliced mushrooms, drained	10 oz.	284 mL
Butter or hard margarine	3 tbsp.	50 mL
Chopped green onions	1/4 cup	60 mL
White wine (or alcohol-free wine)	2 tbsp.	30 mL
Salt	1/4 tsp.	1mL
Pepper, just a pinch		
Onion powder	1/4 tsp.	1 mL
Tarragon	1/4 tsp.	1 mL

Arrange salmon on greased baking sheet with sides.

Stir remaining 8 ingredients in saucepan over medium heat until butter melts. Spoon over salmon steaks. Lay a piece of foil over top. Bake in 450°F (230°C) oven for 10 to 15 minutes per inch (2.5 cm) of thickness until fish flakes with a fork. Serves 4.

CREAMED SALMON

A good quick lunch.

Hard margarine (butter browns too fast)	2 tbsp.	30 mL
Chopped celery	1/2 cup	125 mL
Chopped green pepper	1/4 cup	60 mL
Chopped fresh mushrooms	1 cup	250 mL
Chopped onion	1 tbsp.	15 mL
All-purpose flour	2 tbsp.	30 mL
Salt	1/2 tsp.	2 mL
Pepper	1/16 tsp.	0.5 mL
Milk	1 cup	250 mL
Canned salmon, drained	7 1/2 oz.	213 g
Buttered toast (or toasted English muffin halves)	8	8

(continued on next page)

Melt margarine in frying pan. Add celery, green pepper, mushrooms and onion. Sauté slowly until tender.

Mix in flour, salt and pepper. Stir in milk until it boils and thickens.

Remove skin and round bones from salmon. Flake. Add salmon to frying pan. Stir. Heat through. Add a bit more milk if you would like a thinner filling.

Serve over buttered toast. Makes a scant 2 cups (450 mL). Serves 4.

GOLD RUSH SALMON

Baked in foil, this is wonderfully moist. It is deep orange due to the colorful sweet marinade.

MARINADE

Water	⅓ cup	75 mL
Cooking oil	¼ cup	60 mL
Soy sauce	4 tsp.	20 mL
Rum flavoring	1 tbsp.	15 mL
Mild molasses	2 tsp.	10 mL
Granulated sugar	2 tsp.	10 mL
Salt	1 tsp.	5 mL
Pepper	1 tsp.	5 mL
Garlic powder	½ tsp.	2 mL
Ground ginger	⅛ tsp.	0.5 mL
Salmon, whole dressed	4½ lbs.	2 kg

Marinade: Mix first 10 ingredients in pan or bowl.

Split salmon backbone. Place salmon flesh side down in marinade in refrigerator for about 3 hours. Turn often. Remove from marinade. Wrap in foil. Cook in 400°F (205°C) oven for 25 to 30 minutes until fish flakes easily when fork tested. Serves 6.

Paré Pointer

Southern bees are so well off that every hive has a door buzzer.

FRESH WATER CARP

This has a different flavor when poached in orange juice.

Carp fillets (or Boston bluefish)	1½ lbs.	680 g
Salt, sprinkle		
Pepper, sprinkle		
Butter or hard margarine	2 tbsp.	30 mL
Prepared orange juice	¾ cup	175 mL

Arrange fillets in casserole or small roaster large enough to hold single layer but with no excess space. Arrange with darker side down. Sprinkle with salt and pepper.

Heat butter and orange juice in small saucepan until butter is melted. Pour over fillets. Cover. Bake in 400°F (205°C) oven for about 15 minutes until fish flakes when tested with fork. Serves 4.

CRAB ROAST

This splendid dish has dressing as well as crab. Dressing really adds flavor. Can also be prepared with your catch of the day. Do not freeze.

Hard margarine (butter browns too fast)	1 tbsp.	15 mL
Chopped onion	¼ cup	60 mL
Chopped fresh mushrooms	2 cups	500 mL
Evaporated skim milk (or light cream)	1 cup	250 mL
Salad dressing (or mayonnaise)	1 cup	250 mL
Parsley flakes	2 tsp.	10 mL
Hard-boiled eggs, chopped	2	2
Crabmeat, or other fish or seafood	1 lb.	454 g
CRUMB MIX		
Dry bread crumbs	3 cups	750 mL
Onion flakes	1½ tbsp.	25 mL
Celery flakes	½ tsp.	2 mL
Poultry seasoning	1 tsp.	5 mL
Ground thyme	½ tsp.	2 mL
Salt	½ tsp.	2 mL
Butter or hard margarine	2 tbsp.	30 mL
Reserved crumb mixture	½ cup	125 mL

(continued on next page)

Melt first amount of margarine in frying pan. Add onion and mushrooms. Sauté until soft. Remove from heat.

Add milk, salad dressing, parsley, egg and crabmeat. Stir.

Crumb Mix: Measure next 6 ingredients into bowl. Stir well. Reserve ½ cup. Add to crab mixture. Toss. Turn into ungreased 2 quart (2 L) casserole.

Melt remaining butter in saucepan. Stir in reserved crumb mixture. Spread over casserole. Bake, uncovered, in 350°F (175°C) oven for 30 to 40 minutes until hot. Serves 4 to 6.

BBQ SALMON HANDO

Beautiful golden brown, juicy and full of flavor.

MARINADE		
Cooking oil	½ cup	125 mL
Soy sauce	½ cup	125 mL
White wine (or alcohol-free wine)	1 cup	250 mL
Lemon juice, fresh or bottled	3 tbsp.	50 mL
Honey	¼ cup	60 mL
Garlic powder (or 6 cloves, minced)	1½ tsp.	7 mL
Chopped onion	¼ cup	60 mL
Slices of fresh ginger, thinly cut	4	4
(or ⅛-¼ tsp, 0.5-1 mL ground)		
Salmon, fillets or steaks	1½ lbs.	680 g

Marinade: Measure first 8 ingredients into flat-bottomed bowl. A casserole dish works well. Stir.

Add salmon. Marinate 30 to 60 minutes in refrigerator. Turn often if marinade doesn't cover completely. If using fillets, place skin side down on hot greased barbecue. Close lid. Reduce heat to medium. Allow 10 to 15 minutes cooking time per inch (2.5 cm) of thickness, testing occasionally until fish flakes when fork tested. Remove fillets or steaks with pancake lifter. Remove skin if serving fillets. While salmon is cooking, pour marinade into saucepan. Boil to reduce liquid to half the original amount. Serve over salmon. Serves 4.

PAELLA

Spanish in origin, pie-AY-yuh is a terrific company casserole. Serve with green peas for color contrast.

Cooking oil	2 tbsp.	30 mL
Boneless chicken breast halves	8	8
Chopped onion	1½ cups	375 mL
Garlic cloves, minced (or ½ tsp., 2 mL garlic powder)	2	2
Chorizo or other hot sausage, sliced ½ inch (12 mm) thick	¾ lb.	375 g
Water	4 cups	1 L
Canned stewed tomatoes	14 oz.	398 mL
Long grain rice	2 cups	500 mL
Chicken bouillon powder	4 tsp.	20 mL
Saffron (or turmeric)	¼ tsp	1 mL
Salt	2 tsp.	10 mL
Pepper	½ tsp.	2 mL
Scallops (halve large ones)	1 lb.	454 g
Boiling water to cover		
Medium uncooked shrimp, peeled and deveined	1 lb.	454 g
Boiling water to cover		
Pimiento strips, for garnish		
Black olives, for garnish		

Heat cooking oil in Dutch oven. Add chicken in 1 or 2 batches. Brown both sides quickly. It is not necessary to cook it through at this stage. Remove chicken to plate. Cut in bite size pieces.

Add onion, garlic and sausage to Dutch oven, adding more cooking oil if needed. Sauté until onion is soft.

Add water, tomatoes, rice, bouillon powder, saffron, salt and pepper. Add chicken. Bring to a boil. Cover. Cook over medium heat for about 15 to 20 minutes until rice is tender.

Cook scallops in first amount of boiling water 3 to 5 minutes until white and opaque. Drain. Add.

Cook shrimp in second amount of boiling water for about 1 minute until pinkish and curled. Drain. Add.

Garnish with pimiento strips and olives. Serves 8.

Pictured on page 53.

This is one time the skin is left on every serving. Worth the extra effort it takes to prepare.

Large salmon fillet, quartered lengthwise (tail fillet)	1½ lbs.	680 g
Salt, sprinkle		
Pepper, sprinkle		
Cooking oil	2 tbsp.	30 mL
Ground thyme	¼ tsp.	1 mL
TOMATO SALSA		
Large tomato, seeded and diced	1	1
Parsley flakes	¼ tsp.	1 mL
Lemon juice, fresh or bottled	1 tbsp.	15 mL
Apple juice	¼ cup	60 mL
Hot pepper sauce	¼ tsp.	1 mL
ORANGE ONION SAUCE		
Water	¼ cup	60 mL
Prepared orange juice	2 tbsp.	30 mL
Red wine vinegar	2 tbsp.	30 mL
Chopped green onion	3 tbsp.	50 mL
Beef bouillon powder	½ tsp.	2 mL

Roll up salmon from narrow end, skin side out. Tie with string.

Sprinkle with salt and pepper.

Heat cooking oil in frying pan. Stir in thyme. Add salmon rolls. Cook for about 5 minutes per side on medium-high. Brown each side for about 2 minutes.

Tomato Salsa: Stir all 5 ingredients in small bowl.

Orange Onion Sauce: Stir all ingredients in small saucepan. Bring to a boil, stirring often. Boil until about ½ is evaporated. Spread equal portions on 4 plates on a space that is slightly larger than salmon roll. Set a salmon roll on top. Spoon Tomato Salsa on top of each roll. Serves 4.

BAKED POLLOCK FILLETS

Covering these fillets with tomato slices and mozzarella cheese is most impressive. Seasoning is pleasant.

Alaskan pollock fillets	1¼ lbs	560 g
Salt, sprinkle		
Pepper, sprinkle		
Medium tomatoes, sliced	2	2
Sweet basil	⅛ tsp.	0.5 mL
Garlic powder	⅛ tsp.	0.5 mL
Salt	⅛ tsp.	0.5 mL
Grated mozzarella cheese	1 cup	250 mL

Arrange fillets in baking dish large enough to hold single layer. Sprinkle with salt and pepper.

Lay tomato slices over fillets.

Mix basil, garlic powder and salt together. Sprinkle over tomato slices.

Sprinkle with cheese. Bake, uncovered, in 425°F (220°C) oven for 10 to 12 minutes until fish flakes when tested with a fork. Serves 4.

1. Szechuan Shrimp page 79
2. Sole Special page 55
3. Crab Pasta Rolls page 57
4. Baked Swordfish page 62

Colorful with red and green veggies on top. Very tasty.

VEGETABLE FRY

Cooking oil	1 tbsp.	15 mL
Thin onion slices, quartered	1 cup	250 mL
Small zucchini with peel, cut in short sticks	1	1
Canned stewed tomatoes, drained	14 oz.	398 mL
Canned whole or sliced mushrooms, drained	10 oz.	284 mL
Salt	$\frac{1}{2}$ tsp.	2 mL

FISH

Butter or hard margarine	1 tbsp.	15 mL
Pike fillets (jack fish)	1 lb.	454 g
Salt, sprinkle		
Pepper, sprinkle		

Vegetable Fry: Heat cooking oil in frying pan. Add onion and zucchini. Sauté until soft.

Add tomatoes, mushrooms and salt. Heat through.

Fish: Heat butter in frying pan. Add fish. Brown both sides. Sprinkle with salt and pepper as it browns. Cook until it flakes when tested with fork. Spoon vegetables over top. Serves 4.

FRIED FLOUNDER

This starts out with frying and ends with poaching in wine. Topped with mushrooms and onion.

Hard margarine (butter browns too fast)	1½ tbsp.	25 mL
Chopped onion	1 cup	250 mL
Hard margarine (butter browns too fast)	1½ tbsp.	25 mL
Flounder fillets	1½ lbs.	680 g
All-purpose flour	¼ cup	60 mL
Red wine (or alcohol-free wine)	¼ cup	60 mL
Lemon juice, fresh or bottled	1 tsp.	5 mL
Garlic powder	⅛ tsp.	0.5 mL
Canned sliced mushrooms, drained	10 oz.	284 g

Melt first amount of margarine in frying pan. Add onion. Sauté until soft. Remove onion to small bowl.

Add second amount of margarine to frying pan.

Dip fillets in flour. Arrange in frying pan. Brown underside. Turn fillets. Cook for about 1 minute.

Add wine and lemon juice. Sauté until fish flakes when tested with fork. Transfer fillets to warm platter leaving juice in pan.

Put garlic powder and mushrooms into juice in pan. Stir. Add onion. Heat and stir. Spoon over fillets. Serves 4.

GARLIC MUSSELS

A mussel-lovers dream. Do not freeze.

Mussels	2¼ lbs.	1 kg
Hard margarine (butter browns too fast)	2 tbsp.	30 mL
Garlic cloves, minced	3	3
Ginger root, grated or cut in slivers	2 tbsp.	30 mL
White wine (or alcohol-free wine)	¾ cup	175 mL
Water	¼ cup	60 mL
Grated Parmesan cheese		

(continued on next page)

Tap any open mussels with knife to see if they close. They may take 2 to 3 minutes to close. Discard any that don't close. Scrub mussels, removing beards, with pot scraper. Dip scraper in water often. Rinse mussels.

Melt margarine in large pot. Add garlic and ginger. Sauté for 2 minutes.

Add wine and water. Add mussels. Cover. Boil slowly for 7 to 10 minutes until shells open wide. Discard unopened mussels. Scoop mussels into large bowl. Pour wine mixture over top.

Serve with Parmesan cheese. Serves 3 to 4.

Pictured on cover.

SHRIMP STROGANOFF

Not only beef tastes good in a stroganoff sauce.

Hard margarine (butter browns too fast)	2 tbsp.	30 mL
Medium shrimp, peeled and deveined	1½ lbs.	680 g
Finely chopped onion	½ cup	125 mL
Sliced fresh mushrooms	2 cups	500 mL
All-purpose flour	3 tbsp.	50 mL
Chicken bouillon powder	2 tsp.	10 mL
Salt	½ tsp.	2 mL
Pepper	¼ tsp.	1 mL
Garlic powder	⅛ tsp.	0.5 mL
Paprika	¼ tsp.	1 mL
Parsley flakes	1 tsp.	5 mL
Water	1 cup	250 mL
Sour cream	1 cup	250 mL

Melt margarine in frying pan. Add shrimp. Stir-fry for 3 to 5 minutes until shrimp turns pinkish and curls. Transfer shrimp to bowl.

Add onion and mushrooms to frying pan with more margarine if needed. Sauté until soft.

Sprinkle flour over onion mixture. Add bouillon powder, salt, pepper, garlic powder, paprika and parsley. Mix well. Stir in water until it boils and thickens. Add shrimp. Heat through.

Stir in sour cream to heat but not boil. Makes 4 servings.

BUFFALO SHRIMP

Like Buffalo Wings, but made with shrimp. Can also be served as an appetizer.

Cooking oil	¼ cup	60 mL
Lemon juice, fresh or bottled	2 tsp.	10 mL
Worcestershire sauce	1 tsp.	5 mL
Hot pepper sauce (or more, to taste)	1 tsp.	5 mL
Onion powder	⅛ tsp.	0.5 mL
Garlic powder	⅛ tsp.	0.5 mL
Medium shrimp, peeled and deveined	1 lb.	454 g
Salt, sprinkle		
Pepper, sprinkle		

Stir first 6 ingredients together in medium bowl.

Add shrimp. Let marinate for 30 minutes. Stir often to be sure all shrimp are coated.

Pour shrimp and marinade into baking pan just large enough to hold single layer.

Sprinkle with salt and pepper. Bake, uncovered, in 375°F (190°C) oven for about 5 minutes until shrimp turn pinkish and curl. Serves 2 to 3.

Pictured on page 17.

BROILED SALMON

A very mild sauce is brushed over steaks before broiling.

Lemon juice, fresh or bottled	1 tbsp.	15 mL
Tarragon, generous measure	⅛ tsp.	0.5 mL
Butter or hard margarine	3 tbsp.	50 mL
Salt	¼ tsp.	2 mL
Paprika	⅛ tsp.	0.5 mL
Parsley flakes	¼ tsp.	1 mL
Onion salt	¼ tsp.	1 mL
Salmon steaks	2	2

(continued on next page)

Combine first 7 ingredients in small saucepan. Heat and stir until butter melts.

Arrange salmon steaks on greased broiler pan. Brush with lemon mixture. Broil on second rack from top for about 8 minutes until browned. Turn steaks over carefully. Brush with lemon mixture. Broil about 5 minutes more until fish flakes easily. Serves 2.

Pictured on cover.

MUSSELS AND PURÉE

The purée of vegetables seeps into the mussel shells making a most tasty dish. Do not freeze.

Medium onions, chopped	3	3
Garlic cloves, minced	3	3
Medium tomatoes	2	2
Medium carrots, thinly sliced	3	3
White wine (or alcohol-free wine)	1½ cups	375 mL
Water	1 cup	250 mL
Salt	1 tsp.	5 mL
Pepper	¼ tsp.	1 mL
Whole oregano	½ tsp.	2 mL
Sweet basil	½ tsp.	2 mL
Tarragon	¼ tsp.	1 mL
Parsley flakes	½ tsp.	2 mL
Mussels	4 lbs.	1.8 kg

Combine first 12 ingredients in large saucepan. Cook, covered, until tender-crisp. Drain and reserve juice in bowl. Pour vegetables into blender. Add enough juice to blend smooth.

Tap any open mussels with knife or spoon. They may take 2 to 3 minutes to close. Discard any that don't close. Scrub mussels with pot scraper, removing beards. Dip scraper in water often and rinse mussels. Place in large saucepan. Mix pureé with reserved juice. Pour over mussels. Bring to a boil. Simmer slowly, covered, for 7 to 10 minutes to steam mussels until they open wide. Discard any that don't open. Serves 4.

FRUITED SHARK

Both fish and fruit are cooked on the barbecue. Swordfish or halibut may be used as well. May also be broiled in the oven.

Cooking oil	1 tbsp.	15 mL
Lemon juice, fresh or bottled	1 tbsp.	15 mL
Parsley flakes	½ tsp.	2 mL
Shark fillets	1½ lbs.	680 g
Cooking oil	2 tbsp.	30 mL
Garlic powder	¼ tsp	1 mL
Parsley flakes	¼ tsp.	1 mL

FRUIT
Papaya and/or small cantaloupe,
    halved, peeled and seeded, cut in
    thick slices
Cooking oil

Stir first amount of cooking oil, lemon juice and parsley together in small cup.

Brush over both sides of fillets. Let stand 30 minutes. Cook on greased barbecue.

Mix second amount of cooking oil, garlic powder and parsley together. Brush over fillets as they cook. Cook until fish flakes.

Fruit: Place papaya and/or cantaloupe on greased grill. Brush with cooking oil as you brown both sides. Dice. Serve grilled fish on top of fruit. Serves 4.

Pictured on page 71.

SALMON DORIE

A different flavor and a real treat.

Cooking oil	2 tbsp.	30 mL
Garlic powder (or 2 cloves, minced)	½ tsp.	2 mL
Lemon juice, fresh or bottled	2 tsp.	10 mL
Dijon mustard	2 tsp.	10 mL
Sweet basil (or ¼ cup, 60 mL fresh,	2 tsp.	10 mL
finely chopped)		
Salt	½ tsp.	2 mL
Pepper	⅛ tsp.	0.5 mL
Salmon fillets	1½ lbs.	680 g

(continued on next page)

Stir cooking oil, garlic powder, lemon juice, mustard, basil, salt and pepper together in small bowl.

Lay fillets in baking pan just large enough to hold single layer. Brush with all of garlic-lemon mixture. Marinate at room temperature for 30 minutes or cover and refrigerate for 1 hour. Bake in 450°F (230°C) oven for about 10 minutes per inch (2.5 cm) of thickness until fish flakes when tested with a fork. Serves 4.

Pictured on page 53.

LOBSTER THERMADOR

An old special to eat from the shell of a lobster tail.

Frozen lobster tails (6 oz., 170 g each)	4	4
Boiling salted water		
Hard margarine (butter browns too fast)	1/4 cup	60 mL
Sliced fresh mushrooms	1 cup	250 mL
All-purpose flour	3 tbsp.	50 mL
Salt	1/2 tsp.	2 mL
Pepper	1/8 tsp.	0.5 mL
Paprika	1/2 tsp.	2 mL
Onion powder	1/8 tsp.	0.5 mL
Evaporated skim milk (or light cream), plus milk to make	2 cups	500 mL
Sherry or white wine (or alcohol-free sherry or wine), optional	1 tbsp.	15 mL
TOPPING		
Butter or hard margarine	2 tbsp.	30 mL
Soda cracker crumbs	1/3 cup	75 mL
Grated medium Cheddar cheese	1/4 cup	60 mL

Drop frozen lobster tails into boiling salted water in large pot. Return to a boil. Boil according to package directions or about 8 minutes. Drain. Rinse with cold water. Cut along each underside membrane with scissors and discard. Remove meat carefully and cut into bite size pieces. Set shells aside.

Melt margarine in saucepan. Add mushrooms. Sauté until soft.

Mix in flour, salt, pepper, paprika and onion powder. Stir in milk until it boils and thickens. Add sherry. Add lobster. Stir and heat through.

Topping: Melt butter in small saucepan. Stir in cracker crumbs and cheese. Spoon lobster mixture into lobster shells. Sprinkle with crumb topping. Broil 6 inches (15 cm) from heat for about 3 minutes until browned and bubbly. Serves 4.

OVEN FRIED SEAFOOD

This has a thin coating and very little fat. Can also be used as an appetizer.

Egg whites (large)	2	2
Fine dry bread crumbs	⅓ cup	75 mL
Seasoned salt	½ tsp.	5 mL
Salt	½ tsp.	5 mL
Paprika	¼ tsp.	1 mL
Cayenne pepper	⅛ tsp.	0.5 mL
Shrimp, oysters, scallops, cubed fish fillets	2 lbs.	900 g

Beat egg whites with fork in small bowl until they separate and don't cling together.

Mix next 5 ingredients well in another bowl.

Dip shrimp and/or oysters, scallops and cubed fish fillets into egg white. Coat with crumb mixture. Arrange on greased baking sheet. Bake in 450°F (230°C) oven for about 20 minutes until browned. Serves 6 as a main course.

CLAM FETTUCCINI

Pasta tossed with a tomato clam sauce.

Hard margarine (butter browns too fast)	¼ cup	60 mL
Chopped onion	1 cup	250 mL
Garlic cloves, minced	2	2
White wine (or alcohol-free wine)	¼ cup	60 mL
Canned tomatoes, broken up	14 oz.	398 mL
Dried crushed red pepper	½ tsp.	2 mL
Canned baby clams, with juice	2 × 5 oz.	2 × 142 g
Parsley flakes	½ tsp.	2 mL
Fettuccini	1 lb.	454 g
Boiling water	4 qts.	4 L
Cooking oil	1 tbsp.	15 mL
Salt	1 tbsp.	15 mL

(continued on next page)

Melt margarine in frying pan. Add onion and garlic. Sauté until soft.

Add next 5 ingredients. Stir. Boil slowly, uncovered, for about 30 minutes until slightly thickened. Makes 3 cups (750 mL) sauce.

Cook fettuccini in boiling water, cooking oil and salt in large uncovered pot for 5 to 7 minutes until tender but firm. Drain. Return fettuccini to pot. Add clam mixture. Toss. Makes 7 cups (1.75 L). Serves 6 to 8.

DEEP-FRIED SEAFOOD

Great with French fries on the side.

TEMPURA BATTER

All-purpose flour	⅔ **cup**	**150 mL**
Cornstarch	⅓ **cup**	**75 mL**
Baking powder	**2 tsp.**	**10 mL**
Salt	**1 tsp.**	**5 mL**
Water	¾ **cup**	**175 mL**
Thin fish fillets, such as plaice, sole or cod, cut in triangular shape	**1¼ lbs.**	**560 g**
All-purpose flour	½ **cup**	**125 mL**

Fine dry bread crumbs (see Note)

Fat for deep-frying

Tempura Batter: Measure first 4 ingredients into bowl.

Stir in water to make a thin pancake-like batter.

Dip fillets in flour, then batter. Coat with bread crumbs. Drop into hot 400°F (205°C) fat. Cook until browned. Remove with slotted spoon to paper towel to drain. Serves 4.

Note: Batter without bread crumbs stays crisp for quite a while and is smooth and golden. When coated with bread crumbs, it gets a bit crisper, browns more and stays crisp a little longer. Try both methods.

CIOPPINO

A well-seasoned tomato broth loaded with fish, chup-PEE-noh is a stew.

Olive oil (or cooking oil)	2 tbsp.	30 mL
Chopped onion	1½ cups	375 mL
Small green pepper, seeded and chopped	1	1
Garlic clove, minced	1	1
Chopped celery	3 tbsp.	50 mL
Canned tomatoes, broken up	2 x 14 oz.	2 x 398 mL
Tomato sauce	7½ oz.	213 mL
Small bay leaf	1	1
Whole oregano	½ tsp.	2 mL
Sweet basil	½ tsp.	2 mL
Granulated sugar	1 tsp.	5 mL
Salt	1 tsp.	5 mL
Pepper	¼ tsp.	1 mL
Parsley flakes	1 tsp.	5 mL
Medium shrimp, peeled and deveined, cut in half crosswise	½ lb.	225 g
Rockfish, snapper or cod fillets, cut in bite size pieces	1 lb.	454 g
Scallops, halved or quartered	½ lb.	225 g
Crabmeat, membrane removed	½ lb.	225 g

Heat olive oil in large Dutch oven. Add onion, green pepper, garlic and celery. Sauté gently until soft. Do not brown.

Add next 9 ingredients. Bring to a boil. Simmer slowly, covered, for about 20 minutes. May be made ahead to this point and chilled.

Add shrimp, rockfish and scallops. Return to a boil. Boil about 5 minutes until shrimp is pinkish, rockfish flakes and scallops are opaque. Add crabmeat. Simmer for 3 to 4 minutes to heat through. Remove bay leaf before serving. Makes 9 cups (2.2 L).

Paré Pointer

Sammy's report card was poor in January because they mark everything down after Christmas.

Excellent for a main course and wonderful on an appetizer tray.

Ocean perch fillets, or other fish fillets	1 lb.	454 g
Water to cover		
Large egg	1	1
Salad dressing (or mayonnaise)	2 tbsp.	30 mL
Worcestershire sauce	½ tsp.	2 mL
Sweet pickle relish	1 tsp.	5 mL
Parsley flakes	½ tsp.	2 mL
Salt	½ tsp.	2 mL
Pepper	⅛ tsp.	0.5 mL
Onion powder	½ tsp.	2 mL
Dry bread crumbs	½ cup	125 mL
Milk or water	¼ cup	60 mL
Hard margarine (butter browns too fast)	2 tbsp.	30 mL
Fine dry bread crumbs	⅓ cup	75 mL

Cover fillets with water in saucepan. Bring to a boil. Simmer, covered, for about 5 minutes until fish flakes when tested with a fork. Drain. Cool and flake.

Beat egg with fork in bowl. Add next 9 ingredients. Add fish. Mix well. Let stand 10 minutes so crumbs absorb moisture. Shape into 4 patties.

Melt margarine in frying pan. Dip patties in bread crumbs. Brown patties on both sides. Makes 4 patties.

DEEP-FRIED FISH BITES: Shape mixture into 1 inch (2.5 cm) balls. Beat 2 large eggs and 2 tbsp. (30 mL) water together well with fork. Dip ball in egg mixture. Coat with crumbs. Deep-fry in hot 400°F (205°C) fat until browned. Serve with picks and Seafood Sauce, page 139. Makes 32 to 36.

Unfortunately when a postman gets old he loses his zip.

LOBSTER SPECIAL

A wee bit of curry, a touch of cream cheese and this excellent dish is complete.

Frozen lobster tails (6 oz., 170 g each)	6	6
Boiling salted water		
Butter or hard margarine	¼ cup	60 mL
All-purpose flour	3 tbsp.	50 mL
Salt	½ tsp.	2 mL
Pepper	⅛ tsp.	0.5 mL
Onion powder	⅛ tsp.	0.5 mL
Curry powder	½ tsp.	2 mL
Paprika	¼ tsp.	1 mL
Milk	1 cup	250 mL
Cream cheese, cut up	4 oz.	125 g
Evaporated skim milk (or light cream)	1 cup	250 mL

Drop frozen lobster tails into boiling salted water in large pot. Return to a boil. Boil according to package directions or about 8 minutes. Drain. Rinse with cold water. Cut along each underside membrane with scissors and discard. Remove meat carefully and cut bite size. Set shells aside.

Melt butter in saucepan. Mix in flour, salt, pepper, onion powder, curry powder and paprika. Stir in first amount of milk until it boils and thickens.

Add cream cheese and remaining milk. Heat and stir until cheese melts. Add lobster meat. Heat through. Fill lobster shells. Serves 6.

LOBSTER WITH BUTTER: After lobster tails are cooked, remove meat from shell and cut into bite size pieces. Return to shell. Serve with melted butter as a dip.

Paré Pointer

Behead means that which is connected to a bee's neck.

A meal in one dish topped with mashed potato. An excellent choice.

Cooking oil	2 tbsp.	30 mL
Chopped onion	1 cup	250 mL
Grated carrot (use medium grater)	1 cup	250 mL
All-purpose flour	3 tbsp.	50 mL
Chicken bouillon powder	1 tsp.	5 mL
Horseradish	1 tsp.	5 mL
Salt	1 tsp.	5 mL
Pepper	¼ tsp.	1 mL
Milk	1½ cups	375 mL
Boston bluefish fillets, cut bite size	1 lb.	454 g
Frozen peas	1 cup	250 mL
Medium potatoes, peeled and quartered	4	4
Boiling salted water		
Milk	¼ cup	60 mL
Onion salt	½ tsp.	2 mL
Butter or hard margarine, melted	1 tbsp.	15 mL
Paprika, sprinkle		

Heat cooking oil in frying pan. Add onion and carrot. Sauté until soft.

Mix in flour, bouillon powder, horseradish, salt and pepper. Stir in first amount of milk until it boils and thickens.

Add fish and peas. Cover. Simmer slowly, stirring occasionally, until fish flakes easily. Scrape into ungreased 8 x 8 inch (20 x 20 cm) pan. Set aside.

Cook potatoes in salted water until tender. Drain.

Add second amount of milk and onion salt. Mash. Spread over fish mixture.

Brush potato with melted butter. Sprinkle with paprika. Bake, uncovered, in 400°F (205°C) oven about 20 minutes or until heated through. Serves 4.

TUNA PINWHEEL

An unusual and attractive luncheon dish. Sure to bring lots of comments.

Hard margarine (butter browns too fast)	1 tbsp.	15 mL
Chopped onion	¾ cup	175 mL
Large egg	1	1
Canned tuna, drained and flaked	2 × 6½ oz.	2 × 184 g
Grated medium or sharp Cheddar cheese	¾ cup	175 mL
Chopped fresh parsley (or 1 tbsp., 15 mL flakes)	½ cup	125 mL
Celery flakes, crushed	1 tsp.	5 mL
Dill weed	¼ tsp.	1 mL
Salt	¾ tsp.	4 mL
Pepper	¼ tsp.	1 mL
CRUST		
Biscuit mix	4 cups	900 mL
Milk	⅞ cup	200 mL
Milk for brushing crust	1 tbsp.	15 mL
DILLY CHEESE SAUCE		
Butter or hard margarine	¼ cup	60 mL
All-purpose flour	¼ cup	60 mL
Salt	1 tsp.	5 mL
Pepper	¼ tsp.	1 mL
Dill weed	¼-½ tsp.	1-2 mL
Milk	2 cups	500 mL
Grated medium or sharp Cheddar cheese	1 cup	250 mL

Melt margarine in frying pan. Add onion. Sauté until soft.

Beat egg with spoon in bowl. Add next 7 ingredients. Stir.

Crust: Stir biscuit mix and first amount of milk together in separate bowl to form soft ball. Knead on lightly floured surface 6 times. Roll to 10 × 15 inch (25 × 38 cm) rectangle. Spread with tuna mixture. Beginning at long side, roll up as for jelly roll. Place seam side down on greased baking sheet. Shape into ring, pinching ends to seal. Using scissors, cut from outer edge ⅔ way to center. Make additional cuts at intervals all the way around, making 12 pieces. Lean each piece on its side to allow filling to be seen.

Brush crust with milk so it will brown better. Bake in 375°F (190°C) oven for 25 to 30 minutes.

Dilly Cheese Sauce: Melt butter in saucepan. Mix in flour, salt, pepper and dill weed. Stir in milk until it boils and thickens. Makes 2¼ cups (560 mL) sauce.

Stir in cheese to melt. Spoon over each serving. Serves 6.

Pictured on page 107.

SHRIMP SAUCED CHEESE PIE

A smooth cheesy pie with a shrimp sauce to add the extra touch.

CHEESE PIE

Cream cheese, softened	4 oz.	125 g
Large eggs	4	4
All-purpose flour	3 tbsp.	50 mL
Evaporated skim milk (or light cream)	13½ oz.	385 mL
Salt	½ tsp.	2 mL
Tabasco	⅛ tsp.	0.5 mL
Grated medium Cheddar cheese	¾ cup	175 mL
Grated mozzarella cheese	¾ cup	175 mL
Unbaked 9 inch (22 cm) pie shell	1	1

SHRIMP SAUCE

Butter or hard margarine	2 tbsp.	30 mL
All-purpose flour	2 tbsp.	30 mL
Chicken bouillon powder	1 tsp.	5 mL
Salt	¼ tsp.	1 mL
Pepper	⅛ tsp.	0.5 mL
Dill weed	⅛ tsp.	0.5 mL
Milk	1 cup	250 mL
Canned tiny shrimp, rinsed and drained	4 oz.	113 g

Cheese Pie: Beat cream cheese with 1 egg until smooth. Beat in remaining eggs 1 at a time. Mix in flour. Add milk, salt, Tabasco, and both cheeses. Stir.

Pour into pie shell. Bake in 350°F (175°C) oven for 40 to 45 minutes until an inserted knife comes out clean.

Shrimp Sauce: Melt butter in saucepan. Mix in flour, bouillon powder, salt, pepper and dill weed.

Stir in milk until it boils and thickens.

Add shrimp. Stir. Heat through. Spoon over warm pie wedges. Makes 1½ cups (375 mL) sauce. Serves 6.

CRAB QUICHE

Good and colorful. Can also double as an appetizer when cut in smaller wedges.

Pastry for a 9 inch (22 cm) pie shell, your own or a mix	1	1
Canned crabmeat, drained (or 2 cups, 500 mL fresh), membrane removed	2 × 4.2 oz.	2 × 120 g
Grated medium Cheddar cheese	1 cup	250 mL
Green onions, sliced	3	3
Large eggs	3	3
All-purpose flour	2 tbsp.	30 mL
Dry mustard powder	¼ tsp.	1 mL
Evaporated skim milk (or light cream)	1 cup	250 mL

Roll out pastry and line pie plate. Do not prick holes in it.

Sprinkle crabmeat in shell. Scatter cheese and onion over crabmeat.

Beat eggs, flour and mustard in bowl. Add milk. Stir. Pour over top. Bake in 350°F (175°C) oven for about 40 minutes until set. Serve hot. Serves 6.

Pictured on page 107.

1. Tuna Pinwheel with Dilly Cheese Sauce page 104
2. Seafood Quiche Solo page 111
3. Hot Scallop Salad page 115
4. Crusty Salmon with Red Pepper Sauce page 109
5. Crab Quiche page 106

So different with a red pepper sauce spooned over salmon enclosed in pastry. Rich and good.

Cream cheese, softened	8 oz.	250 g
Onion powder	¼ tsp.	1 mL
Large egg	1	1
Canned sliced mushrooms, drained, finely chopped	10 oz.	284 mL
Salt	¼ tsp.	1 mL
Pepper, sprinkle		
Pastry for a 2 crust pie		
Salmon fillet	1¼ lbs.	560 g
RED PEPPER SAUCE		
Hard margarine (butter browns too fast)	2 tbsp.	30 mL
Red pepper, seeded and finely chopped	1	1
Chopped green onion	¼ cup	60 mL
Evaporated skim milk (or whipping cream)	1 cup	250 mL
Salt	½ tsp.	2 mL
Cornstarch	1 tbsp.	15 mL
Water	2 tbsp.	30 mL

Mix first 6 ingredients well. Set aside.

Roll pastry into size and shape to completely enclose salmon fillet. Spread cream cheese mixture in center of pastry, about the same size as fillet.

Remove skin from fillet. Lay fillet on cream cheese mixture. Dampen pastry edges with water. Bring edges up to center. Seal. Turn pastry-fillet over onto ungreased glass baking dish, seam side down. Pastry bottom will brown better if you use a glass baking dish. Bake in 350°F (175°C) oven about 45 minutes until browned.

Red Pepper Sauce: Melt margarine in small saucepan. Add red pepper and green onion. Sauté until soft.

Add milk. Stir. Bring to a boil.

Mix salt and cornstarch with water in small cup. Stir into sauce until it boils and thickens. Spoon over separate servings. Serves 4.

Pictured on page 107.

IMPOSSIBLE SALMON PIE

When cooked, there will be layers of salmon and peas near the surface. A quick and easy quiche.

Canned salmon, juice reserved	7½ oz.	213 g
Frozen peas, thawed *used broccoli*	1 cup	250 mL
Chopped green onion *& dried onion*	¼ cup	60 mL
Large eggs	4	4
Milk	1½ cups	375 mL
Reserved salmon juice		
Biscuit mix	1½ cups	375 mL

Remove skin and round bones from salmon. Flake salmon. Spread salmon, peas and onion in layers in greased 10 inch (25 cm) pie plate.

Put eggs, milk, salmon juice and biscuit mix into blender. Process until smooth. Pour over salmon mixture in pie plate. Bake in 350°F (175°C) oven for about 40 minutes until a knife inserted halfway between center and outside edge comes out clean. Cuts into 6 wedges.

IMPOSSIBLE CRAB PIE

The finished pie has a top layer of cream cheese slivers. Very easy. A different and rich tasting pie. Cut into smaller pieces for a great appetizer.

Crabmeat (or 1 can 4.2 oz., 120 g, drained), membrane removed	1 cup	250 mL
Grated Gouda or Edam cheese	1 cup	250 mL
Chopped green onion	¼ cup	60 mL
Cream cheese, slivered	4 oz.	125 g
Large eggs	4	4
Milk	1½ cups	375 mL
Salt	¾ tsp.	4 mL
Nutmeg, just a pinch		
Biscuit mix	1½ cups	375 mL

(continued on next page)

Flake crabmeat and sprinkle over bottom of greased 10 inch (25 cm) pie plate. Scatter cheese, then onion and then cream cheese over crabmeat.

Put next 5 ingredients in blender. Process until smooth. Pour over crabmeat mixture in pie plate. Bake in 350°F (175°C) oven for 35 to 40 minutes until a knife inserted halfway between center and outside edge comes out clean. Cuts into 6 wedges.

SEAFOOD QUICHE SOLO

Special food for special people. Keep these in the freezer to pop into the microwave or oven for special times.

Chopped cooked shrimp (or 1 can 4 oz., 113g, rinsed and drained)	¾ cup	175 mL
Finely chopped onion	¼ cup	60 mL
Grated Swiss cheese	1 cup	250 mL
Large eggs	2	2
Milk	⅓ cup	75 mL
Salad dressing (or mayonnaise)	½ cup	125 mL
Salt	¼ tsp.	1 mL
Dill weed	¼ tsp.	1 mL
Pastry for a 2 crust pie, your own or a mix		

Combine shrimp, onion and cheese in bowl.

Beat eggs in small mixing bowl until frothy. Add milk, salad dressing, salt and dill weed. Beat to mix.

Roll out pastry. Cut out twelve 4 inch (10 cm) circles. Fit circles into muffin cups. Divide shrimp mixture among pastry cups. Pour egg mixture over each. Bake in 400°F (205°C) oven for 20 to 25 minutes until browned. Makes 12.

Pictured on page 107.

Paré Pointer

It's a dead ringer. It's a deceased telephone.

SALMON PIE

A lip-smacking savory pie, crusty brown on top, served with a green pea sauce.

Medium potatoes, peeled and quartered	4	4
Chopped onion	1 cup	250 mL
Boiling salted water		
Butter or hard margarine	1 tbsp.	15 mL
Milk	2 tbsp.	30 mL
Canned salmon, (red, such as sockeye, is best for color)	2 × 7½ oz.	2 × 213 g
Pastry for a 2 crust pie, your own or a mix		

SPRING SAUCE

Butter or hard margarine	¼ cup	60 mL
All-purpose flour	¼ cup	60 mL
Chicken bouillon powder	1 tsp.	5 mL
Salt	1 tsp.	5 mL
Pepper	¼ tsp.	1 mL
Milk	2¼ cups	560 mL
Frozen peas	1 cup	250 mL
Reserved salmon	⅓ cup	75 mL

Cook potatoes and onion in salted water until tender. Drain.

Add butter. Mash. Add milk, using a bit more if necessary. Potato mixture should be stiff.

Remove skin and round bones from salmon. Reserve and set aside ⅓ cup (75 mL). Add rest of salmon to potato mixture. Mash well.

Roll pastry and line 9 inch (22 cm) pie plate. Spoon in salmon mixture. Roll out top crust. Moisten bottom edge, lay top crust over filling. Trim and crimp edge. Cut slits in top. Bake in 400°F (205°C) oven for about 30 minutes until browned.

Spring Sauce: Melt butter in saucepan. Mix in flour, bouillon powder, salt and pepper. Stir in milk until it boils and thickens.

Add peas and reserved salmon. Simmer slowly, covered, about 3 minutes until peas are cooked. Spoon over 6 pie wedges.

The topping seals in a tasty filling that has a mild spicy flavor.

CRUST

Butter or hard margarine	6 tbsp.	100 mL
Dry bread crumbs	1¼ cups	300 mL
Onion flakes	1 tbsp.	15 mL
Parsley flakes	1 tsp.	5 mL
Poultry seasoning	½ tsp.	2 mL
Salt, generous measure	⅛ tsp.	0.5 mL
Pepper, just a pinch		

FILLING

Large eggs	2	2
Milk	¾ cup	175 mL
Canned salmon (red, such as sockeye, is best for color), drained	2 × 7½ oz.	2 × 213 g
Dry bread crumbs	1½ cups	375 mL
Grated medium Cheddar cheese	1 cup	250 mL
Onion flakes	1 tbsp.	15 mL
Parsley flakes	1 tsp.	5 mL
Chicken bouillon powder	1 tsp.	5 mL
Prepared mustard	1 tsp.	5 mL

TOPPING

All-purpose flour	1 cup	250 mL
Baking powder	2 tsp.	10 mL
Salt	¼ tsp.	1 mL
Cooking oil	3 tbsp.	50 mL
Milk	6 tbsp.	100 mL

Crust: Melt butter in saucepan. Stir in remaining 6 ingredients. Press into ungreased 9 x 9 inch (22 x 22 cm) pan.

Filling: Beat eggs and milk to blend. Remove skin and round bones from salmon. Flake. Stir salmon and next 6 ingredients into egg mixture. Spoon over crust.

Topping: Measure flour, baking powder and salt into bowl. Stir. Add cooking oil and milk. Stir until it forms a soft ball. Roll or press a bit bigger than pan. Fit over top of filling, pressing crust up sides a bit. Pierce through topping a few places with fork. Bake, uncovered, in 425°F (220°C) oven for about 20 minutes until hot and top is raised and browned. Makes 9 servings.

FISH PIZZA

Very attractive with red and green bits of peppers peeking through the cheese topping. Wonderful flavor.

CRUST

Biscuit mix	2¼ cups	560 mL
Milk	½ cup	125 mL

FILLING

Cooking oil	1 tbsp.	15 mL
Chopped celery	½ cup	125 mL
Chopped onion	1 cup	250 mL
Small red pepper, seeded and chopped	1	1
Small green pepper, seeded and chopped	1	1
Canned stewed tomatoes	14 oz.	398 mL
Garlic powder	¼ tsp.	1 mL
Salt	¼ tsp.	1 mL
Whole oregano	¼ tsp.	1 mL
Cod fillets	1 lb.	454 g
Water, to cover		
Grated mozzarella cheese	2 cups	500 mL
Grated medium Cheddar cheese	½ cup	125 mL

Crust: Mix biscuit mix and milk in bowl to form a soft ball. Press into greased 12 inch (30 cm) pizza pan.

Filling: Heat cooking oil in frying pan. Add celery, onion and peppers. Sauté slowly until soft but not brown.

Add tomatoes, garlic powder, salt and oregano. Boil until most of tomato juice has evaporated.

Cut fillets in bite size pieces. Put into saucepan with water. Bring to a boil. Boil gently about 4 minutes, cooking fish until not quite done. Drain. Spoon ½ tomato mixture over crust. Arrange fish pieces over top. Spoon second ½ tomato mixture over fish.

Sprinkle with mozzarella cheese. Sprinkle Cheddar cheese in center. Bake in 400°F (205°C) oven for about 20 minutes until crust is cooked and cheese is melted. Makes 1 pizza.

This colorful salad is a winner at any table.

Bacon slices, cut in small pieces	4	4
Chopped onion	½ cup	125 mL
Scallops	1 lb.	454 g
Medium zucchini, with peel (7 inch, 18 cm size), sliced diagonally	1	1
Medium tomatoes, chopped	2	2
Water	½ cup	125 mL
Oyster sauce	2 tbsp.	30 mL
Cornstarch	1 tbsp.	15 mL
Romaine lettuce, cut up, lightly packed (increase if desired)	4 cups	1 L
Grated Parmesan cheese, sprinkle		

Sauté bacon and onion in frying pan until bacon is cooked and onion is clear. Transfer to bowl.

If scallops are large, cut in half. Add to frying pan. Sauté until opaque. Add to onion mixture.

Put zucchini and tomatoes into frying pan. Stir-fry until zucchini is tender crisp. Add scallop mixture. Stir.

Mix water, oyster sauce and cornstarch in small bowl. Stir into scallop mixture until it boils and thickens.

Divide lettuce among 4 salad plates. Spoon scallop mixture over top. Sprinkle with cheese. Serve with Blue Cheese Dressing, page 137.

Pictured on page 107.

Paré Pointer

The turkey crossed the road to prove he wasn't chicken.

SALMON FRUIT SALAD

Delight and surprise your friends with this unusual salad.

Canned salmon, drained	2 x 7½ oz.	2 x 213 g
Sliced almonds	¼ cup	60 mL
Oranges, peeled, cut bite size	2	2
Banana, peeled, sliced	1	1
Red apple with peel, diced or sliced	1	1
Torn or cut lettuce, lightly packed	3 cups	750 mL
Salad dressing (or mayonnaise)	¼ cup	60 mL
Milk	1 tbsp.	15 mL
Granulated sugar	½ tsp.	2 mL

Remove skin and round bones from salmon. Flake or chunk. Toast almonds in 350°F (175°C) oven for about 5 minutes. Put salmon and almonds in large bowl with next 4 ingredients.

Mix salad dressing, milk and sugar in small bowl. Pour over salad. Toss lightly. Serves 6.

Pictured on page 125.

TUNA FRUIT SALAD

So fruity mellow. You will think you're eating dessert.

Canned pineapple chunks, drained and cut in half	½ cup	125 mL
Large banana, peeled, sliced	1	1
Sliced or diced celery	½ cup	125 mL
Canned tuna, drained and flaked	6½ oz.	184 g
Salad dressing (or mayonnaise)	2 tbsp.	30 mL
Sweet pickle relish	2 tsp.	10 mL
Milk	1 tsp.	5 mL
Salt	¼ tsp.	1 mL
Paprika	¼ tsp.	1 mL
GREENS LAYER		
Salad dressing (or mayonnaise)	3 tbsp.	50 mL
Milk	2 tsp.	10 mL
Granulated sugar	¼ tsp.	1 mL
Shredded or cut lettuce, lightly packed	4 cups	1 L

(continued on next page)

Combine pineapple, banana, celery and tuna in bowl. Toss lightly.

Mix salad dressing, relish, milk, salt and paprika in small bowl. Add to tuna mixture. Toss lightly.

Greens Layer: Stir salad dressing, milk and sugar together in large bowl.

Add lettuce. Toss. Divide among 4 salad plates or cover 1 large plate. Spoon tuna mixture over top. Makes 2⅔ cups (650 mL) before adding lettuce. Serves 4.

WILD RICE AND SEAFOOD SALAD

Shrimp and crab combined with rice, dressed with a different dressing. Zesty and tasty.

Canned crabmeat, drained, membrane removed	4.2 oz.	120 g
Canned small shrimp, rinsed and drained	4 oz.	113 g
Box of long grain and wild rice, prepared with enclosed envelope as directed on package (such as Uncle Ben's)	6½ oz.	180 g
Chopped green onion	2 tbsp.	30 mL
DRESSING		
Salad dressing (or mayonnaise)	1 cup	250 mL
Red wine vinegar	2 tbsp.	30 mL
Prepared mustard	1 tsp.	5 mL
Prepared horseradish	1 tsp.	5 mL
Frilly lettuce leaves	6-12	6-12
Hard-boiled eggs, quartered lengthwise	3	3
Cherry tomatoes, quartered lengthwise	6	6

Combine crabmeat and shrimp in bowl. Add prepared rice and onion.

Dressing: Stir all 4 ingredients together in small bowl. Pour over rice mixture. Toss. Chill until ready to serve.

Cover 6 salad plates with lettuce. Divide seafood mixture over lettuce.

Arrange egg and tomato wedges around salad on each plate. Serves 6.

Pictured on page 125.

SHRIMP PASTA SALAD

Tomato and shrimp make this salad both a pleasure to the eye and the taste buds.

Rotini	2²/₃ cups	650 mL
Boiling water	3 qts	3 L
Cooking oil	2 tsp.	10 mL
Salt	2 tsp.	10 mL
Hard-boiled eggs, chopped	2	2
Canned tiny shrimp, rinsed and drained	4 oz.	113 g
Chopped celery	½ cup	125 mL
Green onions, chopped	2	2
Tomato, diced	1-2	1-2
Salad dressing (or mayonnaise)	⅓ cup	75 mL
Sour cream	2 tbsp.	30 mL
Granulated sugar	½ tsp.	2 mL
Onion powder	⅛ tsp.	0.5 mL
Salt	¼ tsp.	1 mL

Cook rotini in boiling water, cooking oil and salt in large uncovered pot for 10 to 12 minutes until tender but firm. Drain. Rinse with cold water. Drain well. Return rotini to pot.

Add next 5 ingredients to rotini.

Mix remaining 5 ingredients together in small bowl. Add to rotini mixture. Stir. Makes 6½ cups (1.5 L).

Pictured on page 125.

TUNA CRUNCH SALAD

This salad resembles coleslaw but has additional touches.

Canned tuna, drained and flaked	6½ oz.	184 g
Minced onion	2 tbsp.	30 mL
Sweet pickle relish	3 tbsp.	50 mL
Lemon juice, fresh or bottled	1 tbsp.	15 mL
Grated cabbage (use medium grater)	4 cups	1 L
Salad dressing (or mayonnaise)	¾ cup	175 mL
Potato chips, coarsely crushed	2 oz.	55 g

Put first 6 ingredients into bowl. Mix. Chill until needed.

Just before serving add potato chips. Toss well. Serves 4.

Presentation begins the goodness of this salad. Shrimp on skewers across greens looks so inviting.

MARINADE/DRESSING

Salad dressing (or mayonnaise)	²/₃ cup	150 mL
Milk	2 tbsp.	30 mL
Lemon juice, fresh or bottled	2 tbsp.	30 mL
Worcestershire sauce	1 tsp.	5 mL
Garlic powder	¼ tsp.	1 mL
Seasoned salt	¼ tsp.	1 mL
Large uncooked shrimp, peeled, tails intact, deveined	1 lb.	454 g
Small head of romaine lettuce, cut or torn	1	1
Red pepper, seeded, cut in strips	1	1
Yellow pepper, seeded, cut in strips	1	1
Croutons	½ cup	125 mL
Grated Parmesan cheese	½ cup	125 mL
Reserved marinade	½ cup	125 mL

Marinade: Mix first 6 ingredients together in bowl. Reserve ½ cup (125 mL) for salad.

Thread shrimp on wooden skewers that have been soaked in water for 15 minutes. Brush shrimp with marinade. Arrange close together on tray, marinade side down. Spoon rest of marinade over top. Spoon or brush over shrimp often to keep covered with marinade for 30 minutes. It helps to lay wet paper towels over exposed skewers. Broil or barbecue, turning to cook both sides until pinkish.

Toss next 6 ingredients and as much reserved marinade as needed, together in large bowl. Divide among 4 plates. Lay 2 skewers with shrimp across top of each. Serves 4.

Pictured on cover.

Pâré Pointer

Dr. Jekyll's favorite game is Hyde and Seek.

SHRIMP SALAD

Serve this light-colored salad over leafy green lettuce. Crunchy and delicious.

Long grain rice	1 cup	250 mL
Boiling water	2 cups	500 mL
Salt	1/2 tsp.	2 mL
Finely chopped onion	2 tbsp.	30 mL
Diced raw cauliflower	1 cup	250 mL
Canned broken or small shrimp, rinsed, drained and chopped	4 oz.	113 g
Lemon juice, fresh or bottled	1 tbsp.	15 mL
Salt	1/4 tsp.	1 mL
Salad dressing (or mayonnaise)	1/2 cup	125 mL
Hot pepper sauce	1/4 tsp.	1 mL
Milk	1 tbsp.	15 mL
Granulated sugar	1/4 tsp.	1 mL

Add rice to boiling water and salt in saucepan. Cover. Reduce heat and simmer for about 15 minutes until tender and water is absorbed. Cool.

Add next 5 ingredients to cooled rice in large bowl. Stir.

Mix salad dressing, hot pepper sauce, milk and sugar in small bowl. Pour over rice mixture. Toss. Makes 4 1/2 cups (1.1 L).

HAM AND SHRIMP SALAD

A good mixture with a dill-flavored dressing.

Diced cooked ham	1 cup	250 mL
Small cooked shrimp (or 1 can 4 oz., 113 g, rinsed and drained)	1 cup	250 mL
Chopped celery	1 cup	250 mL
Chopped green pepper	1/2 cup	125 mL
Chopped green onion	1/2 cup	125 mL
Salad dressing (or mayonnaise)	1/2 cup	125 mL
Prepared horseradish	1 tbsp.	15 mL
Dill weed	1 tsp.	5 mL
Salt	1/4 tsp.	1 mL
Pepper	1/8 tsp.	0.5 mL
Shredded lettuce, lightly packed (increase if desired)	5 cups	1.25 L

(continued on next page)

Combine first 5 ingredients in bowl.

Measure next 5 ingredients into small bowl. Stir well. Add to shrimp mixture. Mix carefully. Chill.

Divide lettuce among 6 plates or put all lettuce on a platter. Spoon salad over top. Serves 6.

LOBSTER SALAD

Adding more lettuce allows you to stretch the lobster in this salad. Increase dressing if needed.

SALAD

Cut up cooked lobster meat (or 2 × 5 oz., 2 × 142 g cans, drained, broken up)	**2 cups**	**500 mL**
Sliced celery	**1 cup**	**250 mL**
Hard-boiled eggs, chopped	**2**	**2**
Sliced pimiento stuffed olives	**3 tbsp.**	**50 mL**
Lettuce leaves (whole or shredded)	**4-6**	**4-6**
Alfalfa sprouts	**1½ cups**	**375 mL**

DRESSING

Salad dressing (or mayonnaise)	**½ cup**	**125 mL**
Milk	**2 tbsp.**	**30 mL**
Ketchup	**1 tbsp.**	**15 mL**
Lemon juice, fresh or bottled	**1 tsp.**	**5 mL**
Salt, sprinkle		
Pepper, sprinkle		
Onion powder, just a pinch		
Lemon wedges	**4-6**	**4-6**

Salad: Toss first 4 ingredients together in bowl.

Arrange lettuce on 4 to 6 salad plates. Divide alfalfa sprouts over lettuce. Arrange equal portions of lobster mixture over top of each.

Dressing: Mix first 7 ingredients in small bowl. Spoon over salad.

Serve with lemon wedges. Serves 4 to 6.

CRAB LOUIS

Makes a great luncheon dish. Tart dressing really sets it off.

LOUIS DRESSING

Chili sauce	⅓ cup	75 mL
Salad dressing (or mayonnaise)	⅓ cup	75 mL
Granulated sugar	¼ tsp.	1 mL
Salt	¼ tsp.	1 mL
Prepared mustard	¼ tsp.	1 mL
White vinegar	1 tbsp.	15 mL
Onion powder	⅛ tsp.	0.5 mL
Milk	3 tbsp.	50 mL

SALAD

Small head of lettuce, shredded	1	1
Crabmeat (or 2 × 4.2 oz., 2 × 120 g cans, drained), membrane removed	2 cups	500 mL
Hard-boiled eggs, quartered lengthwise	4	4
Small tomato slices	4-6	4-6

Louis Dressing: Mix all ingredients well in small bowl.

Salad: Divide lettuce among 4 to 6 salad plates. Flake crabmeat. Divide over lettuce.

Arrange egg wedges around edge of plates. Add tomato slice. Drizzle with a bit of dressing. Serve remaining dressing in bowl. Makes 4 to 6 servings.

Paré Pointer

If you have a parrot and a canary, you have birds that know the words and the music.

Bubbly and colorful. Good luncheon idea.

Large egg	1	1
Salad dressing (or mayonnaise)	1/3 cup	75 mL
Lemon juice, fresh or bottled	1 tsp	5 mL
Prepared mustard	1 tsp.	5 mL
Hot pepper sauce	1/8 tsp.	0.5 mL
Crabmeat (or 1 can 4.2 oz., 120g, drained), membrane removed	1 cup	250 mL
Grated medium Cheddar cheese	1 cup	250 mL
Finely chopped celery	1/3 cup	75 mL
Parsley flakes	1 tsp.	5 mL
Green onions, thinly sliced	3	3
Hamburger buns or English muffins, split, toasted and buttered	6	6
Yellow cheese slices, cut round to fit	12	12
Paprika, sprinkle (optional)		

Beat egg with spoon in bowl. Mix in next 4 ingredients.

Stir in next 5 ingredients. Mix well.

Place bun halves on ungreased baking sheet. Spread with mixture. Top each with cheese slice. Broil until bubbly hot and cheese is melted. This will only take 1 to 2 minutes. Makes 1½ cups (375 mL) filling. Use 2 tbsp. (30 mL) per bun half. Makes 12 bun halves.

Pictured on page 125.

CRAB APPETIZERS: Cut each broiled bun into 4 or more pieces.

Do you take your sick bird to get a tweetment?

TUNA FRENCH LOAF

When the hot loaf is sliced, it exposes a tunnel of tuna filling. Good flavor. Do not freeze.

French bread	1	1
Hard-boiled eggs, chopped	4	4
Finely chopped celery	1 cup	250 mL
Canned tuna, drained and flaked	6½ oz.	184 g
Sweet pickle relish	1 tbsp.	15 mL
Chopped pimiento-stuffed olives	1½ tbsp.	25 mL
Onion powder	½ tsp.	2 mL
Garlic salt	½ tsp.	2 mL
Dill weed	¼ tsp.	1 mL
Prepared mustard	½ tsp.	2 mL
Salad dressing (or mayonnaise)	½ cup	125 mL
Dry bread crumbs	⅓ cup	75 mL

Cut bread loaf in half horizontally. With your hand, gently press down along the inside center of the top and bottom loaf halves.

Mix next 11 ingredients together in bowl. Spoon tuna mixture down center of bottom half of loaf. Cover with top half of loaf. Press together gently. Wrap loaf in foil. Heat in 450°F (230°C) oven for 25 to 30 minutes until hot. Cuts into 12 x 1 inch (12 x 2.5 cm) slices.

Pictured on page 143.

1. Seafood Focaccia page 132
2. Shrimp Pasta Salad page 118
3. Wild Rice And Seafood Salad page 117
4. Crab Melt page 123
5. Mock Lobster Rolls page 128
6. Salmon Fruit Salad page 116

SALMON OVEN DOGS

A different twist to these salmon dogs. Convenient to make any time.

Cooked salmon (or 1 can 7½ oz., 213 g, drained)	1 cup	250 mL
Grated medium Cheddar cheese	1 cup	250 mL
Chopped onion, cooked or raw (or ¼ tsp., 1 mL onion powder)	½ cup	125 mL
Sweet pickle relish	1 tbsp.	15 mL
Salad dressing (or mayonnaise)	3 tbsp.	50 mL
Horseradish	1 tsp.	5 mL
Salt	⅛ tsp.	0.5 mL
Hot dog buns, split and buttered	6	6

Remove skin and round bones from salmon. Flake salmon and add with next 6 ingredients into bowl. Stir.

Divide mixture among buns. Use about 3 tbsp. (50 mL) for each bun. Place tops on. Wrap each bun in foil. Refrigerate until ready to heat. Heat in 450°F (230°C) oven for about 10 minutes until hot. Makes a generous 1 cup (250 mL) filling. Makes 6.

TUNA SALAD SANDWICH

A crispy, crunchy sandwich with lots of flavor. Do not freeze.

Canned tuna, drained and flaked	6½ oz.	184 g
Hard-boiled egg, chopped	1	1
Finely chopped celery	½ cup	125 mL
DRESSING		
Salad dressing (or mayonnaise)	6 tbsp.	100 mL
Salt	⅛ tsp.	0.5 mL
Paprika	¼ tsp.	1 mL
Onion powder	⅛ tsp.	0.5 mL
Bread slices, buttered	8-10	8-10

Mix tuna, egg and celery in bowl.

Dressing: Stir first 4 ingredients together well in small bowl. Add to tuna mixture. Stir.

Lay bread slices on working surface. Divide tuna mixture among 4 to 5 slices. Cover with remaining 4 to 5 slices. Makes 1¼ cups (300 mL) filling, enough for 4 to 5 sandwiches.

SALMON BURGERS

These nicely browned burgers are absolutely delicious.

Large egg	1	1
Cooked salmon (or 1 can 7½ oz., 213 g, drained)	1 cup	250 mL
Parsley flakes	½ tsp.	2 mL
Dill weed	⅛ tsp.	0.5 mL
Salt	¼ tsp.	1 mL
Onion powder	¼ tsp.	1 mL
Dry bread crumbs	½ cup	125 mL
Water	¼ cup	60 mL
Hard margarine (butter browns too fast)	2 tbsp.	30 mL
Hamburger buns, split and buttered	4	4

Beat egg with fork in small bowl until blended. Remove skin and round bones from salmon. Mix salmon and next 4 ingredients into egg.

Add bread crumbs and water. Stir well. Let stand 5 minutes so crumbs can soak. Shape into 4 patties.

Melt margarine in frying pan. Add patties. Brown both sides.

Put a patty on bottom half of each bun. Spread patty with Tartar Sauce, page 140. Cover with top half of bun. Makes 4 burgers.

Pictured on page 143.

MOCK LOBSTER ROLLS

A pinkish color. Makes a good lunch.

Haddock, fillets or steaks	1 lb.	454 g
Water, to cover		
Chili sauce	2 tbsp.	30 mL
Horseradish	1 tbsp.	15 mL
Finely chopped celery	1½ tbsp.	25 mL
Salad dressing (or mayonnaise)	3 tbsp.	50 mL
Sour cream	2 tbsp.	30 mL
Salt	⅛ tsp.	0.5 mL
Hot dog buns, split and buttered	8	8

(continued on next page)

Put haddock and water in saucepan. Bring to a boil. Simmer gently for about 5 minutes until it flakes easily. Drain. Cool until you can handle it. Flake the haddock, discarding bones.

Mix next 6 ingredients in bowl. Add fish. Stir. Makes 1½ cups (375 mL) filling.

Spoon about 3 tbsp. (50 mL) into each bun. Makes 8 rolls.

Pictured on page 125.

FISH BURGERS

While these call for salad dressing, you may choose to use Tartar Sauce, page 140.

Cod or sole fillets (about 1 lb., 454 g)	6	6
Lemon juice, fresh or bottled	1 tbsp.	15 mL
All-purpose flour	¼ cup	60 mL
Salt	1 tsp.	5 mL
Pepper	¼ tsp.	1 mL
Paprika	½ tsp.	2 mL
Seasoned salt	¼ tsp.	1 mL
Fat for deep-frying		
Hamburger buns, split, toasted and buttered	6	6
Salad dressing (or mayonnaise),	2-4 tbsp.	30-60 mL
Lettuce leaves, left whole or chopped	6	6

Sprinkle fillets with lemon juice. Set aside.

Stir next 5 ingredients together in small bowl.

Coat fish fillets with flour mixture. Deep-fry in 375°F (190°C) hot fat about 3 to 4 minutes until golden.

Spread top half of bun with 1 to 2 tsp. (5 to 10 mL) salad dressing. Place fish on bottom half of bun. Cover with folded lettuce leaf, or chopped lettuce. Repeat to make 6 burgers.

TUNA BURGERS

Bits of celery manage to make an appearance through the top. Economy plus.

Large egg	1	1
Canned tuna, drained and flaked	6½ oz.	184 g
Dry bread crumbs	½ cup	125 g
Finely chopped celery	⅓ cup	75 mL
Finely chopped onion (or ¼ tsp., 1 mL onion powder)	⅓ cup	75 mL
Salt	¼ tsp.	1 mL
Hard margarine (butter browns too fast)	1 tbsp.	15 mL
Hamburger buns, split and buttered	4	4

Beat egg with fork in bowl. Mix in tuna, bread crumbs, celery, onion and salt. Let stand 5 minutes. Shape into 4 patties.

Melt margarine in frying pan. Add patties. Brown both sides.

Put a patty on bottom half of each bun. Spread patty with Tartar Sauce, page 140, if desired. Cover with top half of bun. Makes 4 burgers.

CRAB SALAD SANDWICH

Looks and tastes yummy. Adding lettuce to the filling makes it crunchy.

Crabmeat (or 1 can 4.2 oz., 120 g, drained), membrane removed	1 cup	250 mL
Salad dressing (or mayonnaise)	⅓ cup	75 mL
Onion powder	⅛ tsp.	0.5 mL
Paprika	¼ tsp.	1 mL
Dill weed	⅛ tsp.	0.5 mL
Lemon juice, fresh or bottled	1 tsp.	5 mL
Parsley flakes	½ tsp.	2 mL
Shredded lettuce, lightly packed	2 cups	500 mL
Bread slices, brown, rye or pumpernickel (or 4 croissants, split), buttered	8	8

(continued on next page)

Mix first 8 ingredients in bowl.

Divide among 4 slices buttered bread. Top with second slice. Cut into 2 or 3 pieces each. Makes about 2 cups (500 mL) filling which is enough for 4 sandwiches.

SHRIMP BUNS

These can be served immediately or chilled in foil until needed. Simply heat foil-wrapped buns in the oven.

Small or medium cooked shrimp (or 1 can 4 oz., 113 g rinsed and drained)	³/₄ cup	175 mL
Grated medium or sharp Cheddar cheese	¹/₃ cup	75 mL
Chopped celery	¹/₃ cup	75 mL
Onion flakes	2 tsp.	10 mL
Salad dressing (or mayonnaise)	¹/₃ cup	75 mL
Parsley flakes	¹/₂ tsp.	2 mL
Hamburger buns, split and buttered	4	4

Combine first 6 ingredients in bowl. Mix.

Spread on bun halves. Arrange on pan. Broil until cheese melts. Makes 1 cup (250 mL) filling for 8 bun halves.

OVEN SHRIMP BUNS: Spread filling on bottom half of bun. Put top on. Wrap each bun in foil. Chill until needed. Bake in 350°F (175°C) oven for 15 minutes until hot and cheese is melted. Makes 4 to 5.

Paré Pointer

A doormat is taken up and shaken but medicine is shaken up and taken.

SEAFOOD FOCACCIA

A super simple snack or, foh-CAH-chee-ah can be served for lunch. This is a dressed up loaf with nowhere to go but to the table.

Cooking oil	2 tbsp.	30 mL
Finely chopped onion	¾ cup	175 mL
Small green pepper, diced	1	1
Diced fresh mushrooms	¾ cup	175 mL
Garlic clove, minced	1	1
Large shrimp, peeled with tails intact, deveined	12	12
Large scallops, sliced in half	12	12
Focaccia herb bread	1	1
Pesto sauce	1 cup	250 mL
Diced black olives or seasoned Italian olives	¾ cup	175 mL
Grated feta cheese	1 cup	250 mL

Heat cooking oil in frying pan. Add onion, green pepper, mushrooms and garlic. Sauté for about 3 minutes.

Add shrimp and scallops. Stir-fry until shrimp turns pinkish and curls a bit and scallops are white and opaque. Remove from heat.

Put focaccia loaf on ungreased baking sheet. Spread with pesto sauce. Mound layer of shrimp-scallop mixture on top. Add olives, then cheese. Bake in 350°F (175°C) oven for 15 to 20 minutes. Serves 2 to 4.

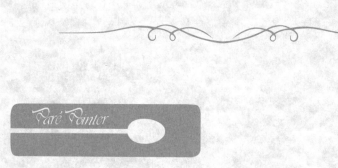

Pictured on page 125.

Pare Pointer

Combine Dracula with a knight from long ago and you have a bite in shining armor.

Melted cheese with bacon — what could be better for a filler-upper?

Cream cheese, softened	4 oz.	125 g
Butter or hard margarine, softened	6 tbsp.	100 mL
Lemon juice, fresh or bottled	1 tsp.	5 mL
Worcestershire sauce	½ tsp.	2 mL
Onion powder	¼ tsp.	1 mL
Crabmeat (or 1 can 4.2 oz., 120 g, drained), membrane removed	1 cup	250 mL
Hamburger buns or English muffins, split	5	5
Tomato slices	10	10
Yellow cheese slices	10	10
Bacon slices	10	10

Beat first 5 ingredients in small mixing bowl until smooth.

Fold in crabmeat.

Divide among bun halves. Spread.

Top with tomato slice, then cheese slice. Arrange on greased baking pan.

Fry bacon until crisp. Cut slices in half crosswise. Do not put bacon on buns yet. Bake buns in 350°F (175°C) oven for 8 to 10 minutes until cheese melts. Place 2 half slices of bacon on top of each bun to serve. Makes a generous 1⅓ cups (325 mL) filling. Makes 10 bun halves using 2 tbsp. (30 mL) each.

Cannibals eat a lot of buttered host for breakfast.

GINGER PEACH SAUCE

A smooth yellow-orange color. A mild, different sauce. Adds conversation to the dish.

Canned sliced peaches, with juice	14 oz.	398 mL
Frozen concentrated orange juice	1 tbsp.	15 mL
Lemon juice, fresh or bottled	1 tbsp.	15 mL
Ground ginger	1/4 tsp.	2 mL
Cornstarch	1 tbsp.	15 mL

Place all ingredients in blender. Process until smooth. Pour into saucepan. Heat and stir until it boils and thickens. Serve over any poached, baked or fried fish fillets. Good spooned over fish steaks as well. Makes 1⅔ cups (400 mL).

SHRIMP SAUCE

Turns any ordinary fish into something special.

Butter or hard margarine	2 tbsp.	30 mL
All-purpose flour	2 tbsp.	30 mL
Salt	1/4 tsp.	1 mL
Pepper	1/8 tsp.	0.5 mL
Chicken bouillon powder	1 tsp.	1 mL
Paprika	1/8 tsp.	0.5 mL
Milk	1 cup	250 mL
Small cooked shrimp (or 1 can 4 oz., 113 g, rinsed and drained)	1 cup	250 mL
Sherry (or alcohol-free sherry)	2 tbsp.	30 mL

Melt butter in saucepan. Mix in flour, salt, pepper, bouillon powder and paprika. Stir in milk until it boils and thickens.

Add shrimp and sherry. Stir. Heat through. Spoon over fried or poached fish fillets. Makes 1½ cups (375 mL).

CREAMY HERB SAUCE

A cream colored sauce flecked with green bits of parsley and dill. Tangy good. Serve hot or cold.

Salad dressing (or mayonnaise)	½ cup	125 mL
Sour cream	½ cup	125 mL
Lemon juice, fresh or bottled	⅛ tsp.	0.5 mL
Chopped chives	1 tbsp.	15 mL
Parsley flakes	1 tsp.	5 mL
Dill weed	½ tsp.	2 mL
Horseradish	1 tsp.	5 mL
Worcestershire sauce	1 tsp.	5 mL

Stir all ingredients together well in bowl or jar. Chill. Serve with fish. If you prefer, mixture may be heated before serving. Makes 1 cup (250 mL).

CREAMED EGG SAUCE

Chicken eggs instead of fish eggs fill this creamy sauce. An old-time recipe. Do not freeze.

Butter or hard margarine	2 tbsp.	30 mL
All-purpose flour	2 tbsp.	30 mL
Seasoned salt	½ tsp.	2 mL
Salt	⅛ tsp.	0.5 mL
Pepper	¼ tsp.	1 mL
Milk	1½ cups	375 mL
Hard-boiled eggs, finely chopped	3	3
Parsley flakes	1 tsp.	5 mL

Melt butter in saucepan. Mix in flour, seasoned salt, salt and pepper.

Stir in milk until it boils and thickens.

Add eggs and parsley. Stir. Serve over fish. Makes a scant 2 cups (500 mL).

CRAB SAUCE

Serve over pasta, toast or in puffed pastry shells.

Butter or hard margarine	2 tbsp.	30 mL
All-purpose flour	2 tbsp.	30 mL
Salt	½ tsp.	2 mL
Pepper	¼ tsp.	1 mL
Garlic powder	⅛ tsp.	0.5 mL
Milk	1¼ cups	300 mL
Canned sliced mushrooms, drained	10 oz.	284 mL
Crabmeat (or 1 can, 4.2 oz., 120 g, drained), membrane removed	1 cup	250 mL
Grated medium Cheddar cheese	½ cup	125 mL
White wine (or alcohol-free wine), optional, but good	1 tbsp.	15 mL

Melt butter in saucepan. Mix in flour, salt, pepper and garlic powder. Stir in milk until it boils and thickens.

Stir in mushrooms, crabmeat, cheese and wine. Heat through. Cheese should be melted. Makes 2 cups (500 mL), enough for 4 servings over pasta.

BUTTERY ONION SAUCE

Goes with any fish or seafood. Simple and quick to make. Adds a finishing touch.

Hard margarine (butter browns too fast)	¼ cup	60 mL
Coarsely chopped onion	2 cups	500 mL
All-purpose flour	2 tbsp.	30 mL
Salt	½ tsp.	2 mL
Pepper	¼ tsp.	1 mL
Water	1¾ cups	425 mL

Melt butter in frying pan. Add onion. Cover and slowly fry until onion is very soft. Do not brown.

Mix in flour, salt and pepper. Stir in water until it boils and thickens. Serve over fish. Makes a scant 2 cups (500 mL).

WHITE SAUCE: Omit onion. Melt butter, mix in flour, salt and pepper. Stir in 1 cup (250 mL) milk instead of water. Serve with any fish.

PARSLEY SAUCE

Just the right sharpness to serve with fish. This can be used instead of a tartar sauce.

Salad dressing (or mayonnaise)	1 cup	250 mL
Red wine vinegar	2 tbsp.	30 mL
Lemon juice, fresh or bottled	2 tbsp.	30 mL
Milk	2 tbsp.	30 mL
Parsley flakes	1 tbsp.	15 mL
Salt	1/2 tsp.	2 mL
Pepper	1/8 tsp.	0.5 mL

Mix all 7 ingredients well. Chill overnight before using so flavors blend. May be served cold as a dip, or warm as a sauce for fish and seafood. Makes 1 2/3 cups (400 mL).

BLUE CHEESE DRESSING

Creamy smooth. A mild blue cheese flavor but with a bit of a bite.

Salad dressing (or mayonnaise)	2/3 cup	150 mL
Sour cream	1/3 cup	75 mL
Crumbled blue cheese	1/4 cup	60 mL
Granulated sugar	1 tsp.	5 mL
Lemon juice, fresh or bottled	1 tbsp.	15 mL
Seasoned salt	1/4 tsp.	1 mL

Measure all ingredients in blender. Process until smooth. Serve with salad. Makes a generous 1 cup (250 mL).

Paré Pointer

If your cat eats a duck you have a duck filled fatty puss.

LEMON SAUCE

A golden sauce just meant for fish.

Brown sugar, packed	2 tbsp.	30 mL
Cornstarch	1 tbsp.	15 mL
Water	³⁄₄ cup	175 mL
Butter or hard margarine	1 tbsp.	15 mL
Salt	¹⁄₈ tsp.	0.5 mL
Lemon juice, fresh or bottled	2 tbsp.	30 mL

Measure sugar and cornstarch in saucepan. Stir well. Mix in water. Heat and stir until it boils and thickens.

Add butter and salt. Stir.

Add lemon juice just before serving. Stir. Serve over fish or on the side. Makes a generous ³⁄₄ cup (175 mL).

DILLED SAUCE

No cooking required. A white sauce with little green flecks showing through. Perfect with fish.

Sour cream	1 cup	250 mL
Salad dressing (or mayonnaise)	1 cup	250 mL
Milk	¹⁄₄ cup	60 mL
Horseradish	1 tbsp.	15 mL
Dry mustard powder	¹⁄₂ tsp.	2 mL
Dill weed	¹⁄₂ tsp.	2 mL
Granulated sugar	¹⁄₄ tsp.	1 mL
Salt	¹⁄₂ tsp.	2 mL

Mix all ingredients well. Serve with any fish or seafood. May be used immediately but flavor is better after refrigerated for an hour. Makes a generous 2 cups (500 mL).

Pictured on page 71.

CURRIED TOMATO SAUCE

A last minute panic sauce that is sure to please. Has a good curry flavor.

Condensed tomato soup	10 oz.	284 mL
Curry powder	1 tsp.	5 mL

Combine soup and lesser amount of curry powder in saucepan. Heat, stirring often, until it starts to bubble. Simmer slowly for 5 minutes. Taste. Add more curry powder if desired. Serve over fried or poached fish. Makes 1 cup (250 mL).

SEAFOOD SAUCE

Shrimp love to be dipped in this tangy sauce. Dark reddish color. Takes moments to make.

Chili sauce	¾ cup	175 mL
Sweet pickle relish	1 tbsp.	15 mL
Horseradish	1 tsp.	5 mL
Worcestershire sauce	½ tsp.	2 mL
Lemon juice, fresh or bottled	¼ tsp.	1 mL

Combine all ingredients in bowl or jar. Chill. Pour into small bowl for serving and dipping. Makes about ¾ cup (175 mL).

RED PEPPER TOPPING

A very different accompaniment for fish. A pretty red color. Do not freeze.

Red peppers, seeded and cut up	2	2
Granulated sugar	1 cup	250 mL
White vinegar	⅓ cup	75 mL

Grind red peppers until finely ground but not puréed.

Stir in sugar and vinegar. Serve with fish or cold meat. Juice is thin. Makes 2 cups (500 mL).

TARTAR SAUCE

Always good served with Fish Burgers, page 129, or deep-fried fish.
Do not freeze.

Salad dressing (or mayonnaise)	1 cup	250 mL
Sweet pickle relish	2 tbsp.	30 mL
Lemon juice, fresh or bottled	1 tbsp.	15 mL
Chopped chives	1 tsp.	5 mL

Stir all ingredients together. Store in refrigerator. Makes 1 cup (250 mL).
Pictured on page 143.

LOBSTER BISQUE

Smooth and very pleasant.

Milk	1 cup	250 mL
Chopped onion	1 cup	250 mL
All-purpose flour	$\frac{1}{3}$ cup	75 mL
Salt	$1\frac{1}{2}$ tsp.	7 mL
Cayenne pepper	$\frac{1}{8}$ tsp.	0.5 mL
Canned lobster, drained	2 × 5 oz.	2 × 142 g
Chopped pimiento	$1\frac{1}{2}$ tbsp.	25 mL
Ketchup	$\frac{1}{4}$ cup	60 mL
Butter or hard margarine	2 tbsp.	30 mL
Milk	5 cups	1.25 L
Evaporated skim milk (or light cream)	$\frac{3}{4}$ cup	175 mL
Sherry (or alcohol-free sherry)	2 tbsp.	30 mL

Measure first 9 ingredients into blender. Process until smooth. Pour
into saucepan.

Add second amount of milk. Heat and stir until it boils and thickens
slightly.

Stir in remaining milk and sherry. Heat through but don't boil. Makes
8 cups (2 L).

Paré Pointer

A coward and linguini gives you a chicken noodle.

Chunky soup with colorful ingredients. So tasty.

Canned stewed tomatoes	14 oz.	398 mL
Chopped onion	1 cup	250 mL
Chopped celery	$^1/_2$ cup	125 mL
Grated potato	1$^1/_2$ cups	375 mL
Grated carrot	$^1/_2$ cup	125 mL
Water	3 cups	750 mL
Milk	$^1/_2$ cup	125 mL
All-purpose flour	$^1/_4$ cup	60 mL
Chicken bouillon powder	1 tbsp.	15 mL
Salt	1 tsp.	5 mL
Pepper	$^1/_8$-$^1/_4$ tsp.	0.5-1 mL
Evaporated skim milk (or light cream)	13$^1/_2$ oz.	385 mL
Canned crabmeat, with juice, membrane removed, flaked	4.2 oz.	120 g

Combine first 6 ingredients in saucepan. Cover. Cook until vegetables are tender.

Measure next 5 ingredients into small bowl. Stir until no lumps remain. Stir into tomato mixture until it boils and thickens.

Add second amount of milk and crabmeat. Heat slowly, stirring often, until steaming hot, but not boiling. Makes 8 cups (2 L).

Pictured on page 143.

TUNA SOUP: Use canned tuna with juice, instead of crabmeat.

A whooping crane is really a stork with pneumonia.

EASY SALMON CHOWDER

A thick and full chowder.

Bacon slices, cut in small pieces	3	3
Chopped onion	1 cup	250 mL
Thinly sliced or diced carrot	¾ cup	175 mL
Chopped celery	¾ cup	175 mL
Water	½ cup	125 mL
Condensed cream of potato soup	2 × 10 oz.	2 × 284 mL
Evaporated skim milk (or light cream)	13½ oz.	385 mL
Salt	¼ tsp.	1 mL
Pepper	⅛ tsp.	0.5 mL
Canned salmon, with juice	7½ oz.	213 g

Fry bacon and onion slowly in heavy Dutch oven until clear and soft.

Add carrot, celery and water. Cover and simmer until tender.

Add potato soup, milk, salt and pepper. Stir.

Remove skin and round bones from salmon. Flake. Add salmon and juice to Dutch oven. Heat slowly, stirring often, until steaming hot, but not boiling. Makes 6⅓ cups (1.6 L).

FISH CHOWDER

Directly from the Atlantic provinces.

Hard margarine (butter browns too fast)	½ cup	125 mL
Chopped onion	1 cup	250 mL
Diced celery	½ cup	125 mL
Green pepper, seeded and diced	1	1
Diced potato	1 cup	250 mL
Boiling water	1½ cup	375 mL
Salt	1½ tsp.	7 mL
Pepper	⅛ tsp.	0.5 mL
Bay leaf	1	1
Haddock fillets (or combination of haddock and lobster), cut bite size	2 lbs.	900 g
Evaporated skim milk (or light cream)	2 cups	500 mL
Granulated sugar	1 tsp.	2 mL

Melt margarine in large saucepan. Add onion, celery and green pepper. Sauté until soft.

Add next 5 ingredients. Cover. Cook until potato is tender crisp. Do not overcook. Discard bay leaf.

Add fillet pieces. Cook for about 5 minutes until fish flakes when tested with a fork.

Stir in milk and sugar. Heat slowly, stirring often, until steaming hot, but not boiling. Makes 8 cups (2 L).

QUICK LOBSTER BISQUE

Fast, good and from the food pantry.

Condensed French Canadian style pea soup	10 oz.	284 mL
Condensed tomato soup	10 oz.	284 mL
Evaporated skim milk (or light cream)	13½ oz.	385 mL
Canned lobster, drained	5 oz.	142 g
Sherry (or alcohol-free sherry)	¼ cup	60 mL

Run all ingredients through blender. Pour into saucepan.

Heat slowly, stirring often, until steaming hot, but not boiling. Makes 4 cups (1 L).

BETWEEN CLAM CHOWDER

Not white like Boston's. Not as red as Manhattan's. But as good as either.

Large potatoes, cubed	3	3
Large carrots, cubed	3	3
Water, to cover		
Bacon slices, diced	10-12	10-12
Chopped onion	1½ cups	375 mL
Chopped celery	1½ cups	375 mL
Large green pepper, seeded and chopped	1	1
Minced clams, juice reserved	2 × 5 oz.	2 × 142 g
Condensed cream of potato soup	2 × 10 oz.	2 × 284 g
Minced clams (from drained can)		
Canned stewed tomatoes	14 oz.	398 mL
Milk	1½ cups	375 mL
Lemon pepper	¼ tsp.	1 mL
Salt	¼ tsp.	1 mL
Pepper	⅛ tsp.	0.5 mL

Combine potatoes and carrots in Dutch oven. Add water. Cover. Cook until tender. Do not drain.

Fry bacon, onion, celery and green pepper in large frying pan until vegetables are soft. Stir often. It is easier to do this in 2 batches. Add to Dutch oven.

Add reserved clam juice and cream of potato soup. Stir often as you bring mixture to a boil and simmer gently for 10 to 15 minutes.

Add remaining 6 ingredients. Stir. Heat slowly, stirring often, until steaming hot, but not boiling. Makes 13½ cups (3.3 L).

Care Pointer

A great many kitchens are accident prone and a great many families eat them.

QUICK CRAB BISQUE

A comforting soup from the shelf. No one can guess how it is made.
Pumpkin colored and smooth.

Condensed green pea soup	10 oz.	284 mL
Condensed tomato soup	10 oz.	284 mL
Evaporated skim milk (or light cream)	13½ oz.	385 mL
Condensed beef consommé	10 oz.	284 mL
Crabmeat (or use 1 can 4.2 oz., 120 g, drained), membrane removed	1 cup	250 g
Milk	⅔ cup	150 mL
Pepper, just a pinch		
Ground mace	½ tsp.	2 mL

Combine all ingredients in heavy saucepan or top of double boiler. Heat slowly, stirring often, until steaming hot, but not boiling. Makes 6⅔ cups (1.5 L).

SIMPLE CRAB SOUP

Creamy white with a mild and delicious flavor.

Butter or hard margarine	⅓ cup	75 mL
All-purpose flour	⅓ cup	75 mL
Chicken bouillon powder	1 tbsp.	15 mL
Pepper (white is best for color)	⅛ tsp.	0.5 mL
Milk	4 cups	1 L
Crabmeat (or 1 can 4.2 oz., 120 g drained), membrane removed	1 cup	250 mL
Sherry (or alcohol-free sherry)	1½ tbsp.	25 mL
Chopped chives, for garnish		

Melt butter in saucepan. Mix in flour, bouillon powder and pepper. Stir in milk until it boils and thickens.

Add crabmeat and sherry. Heat through but do not boil.

Sprinkle each serving with chives. Makes 5 cups (1.25 L).

A CINCH CLAM CHOWDER

Good, thick and tasty.

Bacon slices, diced	2-3	2-3
Chopped onion	¼ cup	60 mL
Water	1 cup	250 mL
Milk	1½ cups	375 mL
Canned minced or chopped clams, with juice	2 × 5 oz.	2 × 142 g
Instant potato flakes	1½ cups	375 mL
Evaporated skim milk (or light cream)	¾ cup	175 mL
Chicken bouillon powder	1 tbsp.	15 mL
Chopped chives, for garnish		

Sauté bacon and onion slowly in large saucepan until onion is soft.

Add water and first amount of milk. Bring to a boil, stirring often.

Add clams with juice, potato flakes, remaining milk and bouillon powder. Heat and stir until it returns to a simmer. Simmer for 5 minutes.

Sprinkle each bowlful with chives. Makes 5¼ cups (1.3 L).

CREAMY TURBOT SOUP

An orangy beige color with a hint of tomato. Excellent flavor. This soup is also excellent using cod.

Water	5 cups	1.25 L
Chicken bouillon powder	2 tbsp.	30 mL
Turbot fillets	1 lb.	454 g
Coarsely chopped carrot	1 cup	250 mL
Coarsely chopped celery	½ cup	125 mL
Coarsely chopped onion	1 cup	250 mL
Medium tomato, cut up	1	1
All-purpose flour	3 tbsp.	50 mL
Salt	½ tsp.	2 mL
Pepper	¼ tsp.	1 mL
Ground thyme	¼ tsp.	1 mL
Evaporated skim milk (or light cream)	13½ oz.	385 mL
Milk	⅔ cup	150 mL

(continued on next page)

Bring water and bouillon powder to a boil in large saucepan. Add fillets. Cover. Simmer gently until fish barely flakes. Remove with slotted spoon to plate. Cool.

Add carrot, celery, onion and tomato to fish broth in saucepan. Cover. Simmer slowly for 20 to 30 minutes until tender. Remove vegetables with slotted spoon to blender.

Add flour, salt, pepper and thyme to blender. Process until smooth. Stir into hot broth.

Add both milks. Heat and stir until it boils and thickens. Flake fish into small pieces. Add. Heat through. Makes $9\frac{1}{3}$ cups (2.2 L).

Pictured on page 143.

═══ MANHATTAN CLAM CHOWDER ═══

A good variation of clam chowder. Reddish orange in color and tastes very good.

Bacon slices, diced	4	4
Chopped onion	1 cup	250 mL
Medium potatoes, peeled and diced	2	2
Canned tomatoes, broken up	14 oz.	398 mL
Finely diced celery	1 cup	250 mL
Chicken bouillon powder	1 tbsp.	15 mL
Salt	$\frac{1}{2}$ tsp.	2 mL
Pepper	$\frac{1}{4}$ tsp.	1 mL
Ground thyme	$\frac{1}{4}$ tsp.	1 mL
Cayenne pepper (optional but good)	$\frac{1}{8}$ tsp.	0.5 mL
Water	3 cups	750 mL
All-purpose flour	$\frac{1}{4}$ cup	60 mL
Water	1 cup	250 mL
Canned baby clams, with juice, chopped	5 oz.	142 g

Fry bacon and onion in large Dutch oven until bacon is cooked and onion is clear.

Add next 9 ingredients. Bring to a boil. Boil gently, covered, for about 25 minutes until vegetables are tender.

Mix flour and second amount of water until smooth. Stir into boiling mixture until it returns to a boil and thickens.

Add clams and juice. Heat through. Makes $7\frac{1}{3}$ cups (1.8 L).

Pictured on page 143.

NEW ENGLAND CLAM CHOWDER

Darkish creamy soup with vegetables showing. Thick and yummy.

Medium potatoes, peeled and diced	3	3
Finely chopped celery	½ cup	125 mL
Grated carrot	1 cup	250 mL
Water	1 cup	250 mL
Bacon slices, diced	3	3
Chopped onion	1½ cups	375 mL
Butter or hard margarine	3 tbsp.	50 mL
All-purpose flour	½ cup	125 mL
Salt	1 tsp.	5 mL
Pepper	⅛ tsp.	0.5 mL
Milk	2 cups	500 mL
Evaporated skim milk (or 1½ cups, 375 mL, light cream)	13½ oz.	385 mL
Cream style corn	½ cup	125 mL
Canned baby clams, with juice, chopped	5 oz.	142 g

Put first 4 ingredients into large saucepan. Cover and simmer for about 20 minutes until tender. Do not drain.

Fry bacon and onion in large frying pan until bacon is cooked and onion is clear.

Add butter, flour, salt and pepper to bacon and onion. Mix in. Stir in first amount of milk until it boils and thickens. Stir into vegetable mixture in saucepan.

Add evaporated milk, corn and clams. Heat slowly, stirring often, until steaming hot, but not boiling. Makes 8 cups (2 L).

Paré Pointer

A cat's favorite breakfast is mice crispies.

Throughout this book measurements are given in Conventional and Metric measure. To compensate for differences between the two measurements due to rounding, a full metric measure is not always used. The cup used is the standard 8 fluid ounce. Temperature is given in degrees Fahrenheit and Celsius. Baking pan measurements are in inches and centimetres as well as quarts and litres. An exact metric conversion is given below as well as the working equivalent (Standard Measure).

OVEN TEMPERATURES

Fahrenheit (°F)	Celsius (°C)
175°	80°
200°	95°
225°	110°
250°	120°
275°	140°
300°	150°
325°	160°
350°	175°
375°	190°
400°	205°
425°	220°
450°	230°
475°	240°
500°	260°

SPOONS

Conventional Measure	Metric Exact Conversion Millilitre (mL)	Metric Standard Measure Millilitre (mL)
1/4 teaspoon (tsp.)	1.2 mL	1 mL
1/2 teaspoon (tsp.)	2.4 mL	2 mL
1 teaspoon (tsp.)	4.7 mL	5 mL
2 teaspoons (tsp.)	9.4 mL	10 mL
1 tablespoon (tbsp.)	14.2 mL	15 mL

CUPS

1/4 cup (4 tbsp.)	56.8 mL	50 mL
1/3 cup (5 1/3 tbsp.)	75.6 mL	75 mL
1/2 cup (8 tbsp.)	113.7 mL	125 mL
2/3 cup (10 2/3 tbsp.)	151.2 mL	150 mL
3/4 cup (12 tbsp.)	170.5 mL	175 mL
1 cup (16 tbsp.)	227.3 mL	250 mL
4 1/2 cups	1022.9 mL	1000 mL (1 L)

PANS

Conventional Inches	Metric Centimetres
8x8 inch	20x20 cm
9x9 inch	22x22 cm
9x13 inch	22x33 cm
10x15 inch	25x38 cm
11x17 inch	28x43 cm
8x2 inch round	20x5 cm
9x2 inch round	22x5 cm
10x4 1/2 inch tube	25x11 cm
8x4x3 inch loaf	20x10x7 cm
9x5x3 inch loaf	22x12x7 cm

DRY MEASUREMENTS

Conventional Measure Ounces (oz.)	Metric Exact Conversion Grams (g)	Metric Standard Measure Grams (g)
1 oz.	28.3 g	30 g
2 oz.	56.7 g	55 g
3 oz.	85.0 g	85 g
4 oz.	113.4 g	125 g
5 oz.	141.7 g	140 g
6 oz.	170.1 g	170 g
7 oz.	198.4 g	200 g
8 oz.	226.8 g	250 g
16 oz.	453.6 g	500 g
32 oz.	907.2 g	1000 g (1 kg)

CASSEROLES (Canada & Britain)

Standard Size Casserole	Exact Metric Measure
1 qt. (5 cups)	1.13 L
1 1/2 qts. (7 1/2 cups)	1.69 L
2 qts. (10 cups)	2.25 L
2 1/2 qts. (12 1/2 cups)	2.81 L
3 qts. (15 cups)	3.38 L
4 qts. (20 cups)	4.5 L
5 qts. (25 cups)	5.63 L

CASSEROLES (United States)

Standard Size Casserole	Exact Metric Measure
1 qt. (4 cups)	900 mL
1 1/2 qts. (6 cups)	1.35 L
2 qts. (8 cups)	1.8 L
2 1/2 qts. (10 cups)	2.25 L
3 qts. (12 cups)	2.7 L
4 qts. (16 cups)	3.6 L
5 qts. (20 cups)	4.5 L

INDEX

154

MAIL ORDER FORM

Deduct $5.00 for every $35.00 ordered

Save $5.00

COMPANY'S COMING SERIES

ENGLISH

Quantity		Quantity		Quantity	
	150 Delicious Squares		Vegetables		Microwave Cooking
	Casseroles		Main Courses		Preserves
	Muffins & More		Pasta		Light Casseroles
	Salads		Cakes		Chicken, Etc.
	Appetizers		Barbecues		Kids Cooking *NEW*
	Desserts		Dinners of the World		Fish & Seafood *NEW*
	Soups & Sandwiches		Lunches		Breads (September '96)
	Holiday Entertaining		Pies		
	Cookies		Light Recipes		

	NO. OF BOOKS	PRICE
FIRST BOOK: $12.99 + $3.00 shipping = **$15.99 each** x		= $
ADDITIONAL BOOKS: $12.99 + $1.50 shipping = **$14.49 each** x		= $

PINT SIZE BOOKS

Quantity		Quantity		Quantity	
	Finger Food		Buffets	*NEW*	Chocolate
	Party Planning		Baking Delights		

	NO. OF BOOKS	PRICE
FIRST BOOK: $4.99 + $2.00 shipping = **$6.99 each** x		= $
ADDITIONAL BOOKS: $4.99 + $1.00 shipping = **$5.99 each** x		= $

JEAN PARÉ LIVRES DE CUISINE

FRENCH

Quantity		Quantity		Quantity	
	150 délicieux carrés		Délices des fêtes		Les casseroles légères
	Les casseroles		Recettes légères		Poulet, etc.
	Muffins et plus		Les salades		La cuisine pour les enfants
	Les dîners		La cuisson au micro-ondes		Poissons et fruits de mer *NEW*
	Les barbecues		Les pâtes		Les pains (septembre '96) *NEW*
	Les tartes		Les conserves		

	NO. OF BOOKS	PRICE
FIRST BOOK: $12.99 + $3.00 shipping = **$15.99 each** x		= $
ADDITIONAL BOOKS: $12.99 + $1.50 shipping = **$14.49 each** x		= $

TOTAL

- **MAKE CHEQUE OR MONEY ORDER PAYABLE TO:** *COMPANY'S COMING PUBLISHING LIMITED*

- **ORDERS OUTSIDE CANADA:** *Must be paid in U.S. funds by cheque or money order drawn on Canadian or U.S. bank.*

- *Prices subject to change without prior notice.*

- *Sorry, no C.O.D.'s*

TOTAL PRICE FOR ALL BOOKS	$
Less $5.00 for every $35.00 ordered −	$
SUBTOTAL	$
Canadian residents add G.S.T. +	$
TOTAL AMOUNT ENCLOSED	$

Please complete shipping address on reverse.

Gift Giving

- Let us help you with your gift giving!

- We will send cookbooks directly to the recipients of your choice if you give us their names and addresses.

- Be sure to specify the titles you wish to send to each person.

- If you would like to include your personal note or card, we will be pleased to enclose it with your gift order.

- Company's Coming Cookbooks make excellent gifts. Birthdays, bridal showers, Mother's Day, Father's Day, graduation or any occasion... collect them all!

Shipping address

Send the Company's Coming Cookbooks listed on the reverse side of this coupon, to:

Name:

Street:

City: Province/State:

Postal Code/Zip: Tel: (   )   —

Company's Coming
COOKBOOKS

Company's Coming Publishing Limited
Box 8037, Station F
Edmonton, Alberta, Canada T6H 4N9
Tel: (403) 450-6223
Fax: (403) 450-1857

Sample Recipe from
Breads

ANADAMA BREAD

A bread with a long history from pioneer days.

Boiling water	2 cups	500 mL
Cornmeal	½ cup	125 mL
Butter or hard margarine	3 tbsp.	50 mL
Mild molasses	½ cup	125 mL
Salt	2 tsp.	10 mL
Warm water	½ cup	125 mL
Granulated sugar	1 tsp.	5 mL
Envelope active dry yeast	1 x ¼ oz.	1 x 8 g
All-purpose flour	2 cups	500 mL
All-purpose flour	4½ cups	1 L
Melted butter	2 tsp.	10 mL
Cornmeal	2 tbsp.	30 mL

Gradually stir boiling water into first amount of cornmeal in mixing bowl. Add butter, molasses and salt. Stir well. Set aside to cool to lukewarm.

Stir remaining water and sugar together in cup to dissolve sugar. Sprinkle with yeast. Let stand 10 minutes. Stir to dissolve yeast. Add to cornmeal mixture. Mix.

Add first amount of flour. Beat on low until moistened. Beat on medium about 2 minutes.

Stir in remaining flour to make a soft dough. Turn out onto lightly floured surface. Knead for 8 to 10 minutes until smooth and elastic. Place in large greased bowl, turning so top is greased. Cover with dry dish towel. Let stand in warm, draft-free location for about 1 to 1½ hours until dough has doubled in size. Turn out onto lightly floured surface. Divide into 2 equal portions. Knead dough down to get rid of air bubbles and shape into 2 loaves. Sprinkle bottoms of 2 greased 9 x 5 inch (22 x 12 cm) pans with 1 tbsp. (15 mL) cornmeal, reserving the second tablespoon for topping. Cover with dish towel. Let rise for about 30 to 45 minutes, until doubled in size.

Gently brush tops with melted butter. Sprinkle with cornmeal. Bake in 375°F (190°C) oven for 35 to 45 minutes until bread sounds hollow when tapped on bottom of loaf. Remove from pans to rack. Cool. Makes 2 loaves.